May I
all t
at

Healing Plants and Animals from a Distance

Curative Principles and Applications

Jim PathFinder Ewing
(Nvnehi Awatisgi)

FINDHORN PRESS

(handwritten annotations)

May I all t at

Then ^ check in Thanks

②

Learn to Listen See Be

raise vibrate by check in

May I connect to all being of Light to assist me? Then check in

③ May I perform healing for the highest good? Then chalk in

(144)

④ may I connect to animal/plant for healing / Health wholeness

First published by Findhorn Press 2007

ISBN 978-1-84409-111-9

Edited by Howard I Wells
Proof-read by Shari Mueller
Cover design by Damian Keenan
Illustrations by Annette Waya Ewing
Layout by Pam Bochel
Printed in the USA

1 2 3 4 5 6 7 8 9 10 11 12 13 12 11 10 09 08 07

*A portion of the author's proceeds from the sale of each book will be
donated to Native American and other organizations dedicated to
spiritual teachings.*

Published by
Findhorn Press
305A The Park,
Findhorn, Forres
Scotland IV36 3TE

Tel 01309 690582
Fax 01309 690036
email: info@findhornpress.com
www.findhornpress.com

Is this your energy
Is this your Belief
System?

To the Plant and Animal Nations
of the Earthly Mother
who share our world
as Children of Earth and Sky

What will I
gain from Letting go

How can I find Balance
in this moment

What can wait until
Tomorrow to have my
full attention

What are 3 ways I made
myself proud

What issue can I lay to rest
now

In the Great Mandala of the Earth,
There are many beings,
Seen and unseen, known and unknown,
But among them, we are Children of Earth & Sky
Our feet as prayers, our words as whispers
One with all

Imagine

creator enrgy
↓

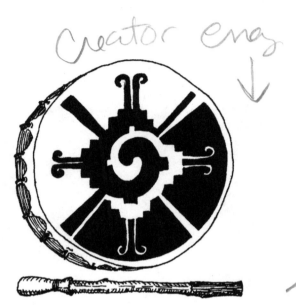

earth energy ↑

Faith
Above me
Grace Below me
Light within me
Peace Around me

Contents

Preface

The Plant and Animal Nations

The Indian prefers the soft sound of the wind
darting over the face of the pond, the smell of
the wind itself cleansed by a midday rain. ...
The air is precious to the red man, for all
things are the same breath — the animals,
the trees, the man.

— CHIEF SEATTLE
SUQUAMISH 1786–1866

Traditional Native Americans speak of the plant and animal "nations" because it gives respect to plants and animals by recognizing their sovereignty. Each plant, each animal, has its own being, its own life and its own purpose in the scheme of Creation, is loved by Creator and has Creator within it, the spark of life, or "good medicine" that makes it so. The classes of plants and animals all have their rights and responsibilities, their reasons for being and their authority to be here.

This understanding of nature is quite different from the Western view where we speak of man vs. nature, or "the environment," as if it was something separate from us.

In a balanced view of the world, we do not have "dominion" over plants and animals; we coexist with them. We are related to them and we honor and respect the sacredness of their lives and being, as we honor our own life and being. We acknowledge that we cannot live upon this Earth without them — for our food, shelter, clothing, medicines — and never lose sight of this important relationship, especially when we must kill them. We are all Children of Earth and Sky; to lose sight of this fact diminishes our own sacredness.

It is in exploring this sacredness that we learn to heal... to make whole, and in harmony; that is the basis of healing. In learning to live with the plant and animal nations in harmony, in dialogue, where we each give and receive, we find wholeness, healing. Finding this dialogue, this connection, a way of balance and harmony, is the purpose of this book. We have much to learn from both the plant and animal nations and the peoples who have come before us.

The plants and animals of the Earth freely give of themselves so that we may live. If you learn to dialogue with plants and animals, you will find that they don't mind sacrificing themselves so that we may eat and have shelter and clothing; only that we gather them responsibly, with respect, so that they may continue to thrive. In the balance of nature, they do the same. It is all part of the chances and choices of survival, balancing the one against the other, for the sake of all. We can learn much from the indigenous peoples who trod this same ground before us, breathing the same air, specifically in their relationships with plants and animals. In Native way, when consuming plants or animals for food, we give thanks — heartfelt prayers of gratitude — for their sacrifice. The act of giving such thanks blesses the food energetically so that it may become "one" with us for health, growth and nurturing.[1]

This respectful attitude and way of living in balance and harmony with the plant and animal nations, called living in "right relation," is vital for today if we are to sustain the planet. The Native American peoples, and other indigenous cultures throughout the world provide us with both spiritual and practical lessons in living in right relation.

For example, in a practical way, when the first Europeans came to the Americas, they were amazed at the park-like qualities of the forests. Native Americans routinely practiced controlled burning to keep brush down and prevent the devastating forest fires from deadwood that would kill animals and destroy villages. They kept meadows and fields open by burning, as well; but they didn't slash and burn as Europeans did, but rather used a process called slash and char. Early Americans didn't completely burn the vegetable matter, but scorched it to make charcoal and then stirred the charcoal into the soil creating what's called *terra preta* throughout the Americas. This process used low intensity fires — reportedly so cool they could be walked through — that would improve the soil and make better, more efficient use of the carbon in the plants. As a result of this carefully cultivated, low-biomass fire-making, the soil was left with more plant-available phosphorus, calcium, sulphur and nitrogen — often with rich, black, fertile soil layers up to six feet deep. They also worked in turtle, fish and animal bones, building fertile humus. In contrast, conventional modern growing methods destroy humus, so it has to be constantly replaced and amended with chemicals. The Native American's process also didn't release as much carbon into the atmosphere, a key cause of our current climate change.[2]

In addition, Native Americans were remarkable bioengineers. Their most noted produce — corn or maize — is unique to the Americas; there is nothing like it anywhere else on Earth. Agronomists are amazed that indigenous peoples of the Americas could cultivate it, for in its original form, it was a relatively rare mountain plant with small fruit and a tough husk that required considerable knowledge and patience to develop. They were expert nutritionists, as well: with squash and beans, maize provided a nutritionally complete, balanced diet that was centuries ahead of the nutritional standards of the Europeans.[3]

Agronomists have determined there are at least 50,000 potential variants of maize, with hundreds of varieties once cultivated, from hand-sized cobs of a single color, to two-foot cobs of many colors, each with a different use and method of preparation. With maize came the Native way of planting in the *milpa,* or plot, set aside for each strain. The Three Sisters — corn, beans and squash — were planted so that the runners could go up the corn stalk and find sunlight and the legumes could at the same time enrich the soil with nitrogen.[4]

In this way, fields would never go barren, with continuous crops on the same fields for centuries and yields-per-acre actually increasing as these fields were used. When the first Europeans exported maize, those who grew it didn't follow the *milpa* method, and hence received sustenance but not the balanced diet that squash and beans gave, resulting in pellagra and fields that grew barren.

This short-sighted agricultural practice continues today at an accelerated pace. American corporations export only a handful of corn seeds, hybrids that produce only one type, size and color and require the chemical support of fertilizers, fungicides and pesticides throughout the growing period. The hybrids cannot reproduce, so they must be ordered from the manufacturer each year. These unnatural monocultures are uniquely fragile with no natural immunity to insects or pathogens. As such, they require increasingly strong/toxic chemical protection that further diminishes the soil and pollutes the air and water, upsetting the ecosystem in a domino-like effect in ways that are far too complex and far-reaching for scientists to predict. In both soil conservation and natural propagation of species, there literally is no "seed corn" for future generations.

We of the West haven't really "advanced" what was taught by the ancestors of this land. We have practiced a different way and called it progress. We are however, beginning to understand we must reconnect with the plant and animal nations for ourselves, our world and future generations. And here is where the practical marries with the spiritual. Native Americans did not separate the material world from the spiritual world. Indeed, in Native way, the physical world springs from the spiritual; in effect, the spiritual is "more real" than the "real" world... a giant departure from the modern view of the world. This is probably the greatest lesson we might learn: bringing the nations — plant, animal, human — together through right relationship.

While science — which divorces the physical from the spiritual — has increased yields per acre substantially, we have paid a price in our spiritual relationships with the land, the plant and animal nations, our planet and ourselves. We live in a world out of balance that must be changed now, if we are to survive. The imbalanced state of the world can be seen as a reflection of our own disconnect with nature, and the change must come from within. It starts with living in balance with all our relations as individuals and as a culture: respecting ourselves, our plant and animal relations and Earth herself.

Modern life is not intrinsically averse to living in balance with the plant nations; far from it. Native Americans have shown us that the technology of sustainable living by honoring Earth and the plant nations can be a more efficient, scientifically valid way of life that has physical, spiritual, emotional and psychological benefits. Human beings actually feel their loss of connection with nature. The term "biophilia" was coined by Pulitzer Prize winning author and Harvard biologist Edward O. Wilson in 1984 as the title of a book by the same name.[5] He argued that this feeling of loss with "the connections that human beings subconsciously seek with the rest of life" is determined by a biological need cultivated over millennia that is not merely a physical bond, but a psychological and spiritual bond, as well. This hypothesis was bolstered by a 2001 article in *American Journal of Preventive Medicine* by Howard Frumkin, MD, an associate professor and chairman of environmental and occupational health at Emory University, who cited studies regarding health and proximity to plants and animals — even if the proximity were only a prison cell window facing a field.[6] The need for oneness — for spiritual and physical connection — among all beings is intrinsic to the human condition.

The ancestors showed us that right relationship is a symbiosis of respect for the land, the people and all beings, demonstrated in the physical and spiritual worlds, for they are one. Right relationship between the human, plant and animal nations is desperately needed in bringing balance to the Earth today. Each one of us can help fulfill this need by recognizing the necessity for change and supporting organizations and activities that promote sustainable agriculture, as well as through rejecting (as much as possible) modern food "processing", which dehumanizes the plant/animal/human relationship and despoils our planet.[7]

On a more personal level, listen to your body. It feels the loss through lack of well-being, physical imbalance and stress caused by pesticides, chemicals, added hormones and genetically engineered species that do not "speak" to our bodies and hold a healing dialogue. No matter how diligently and prayerfully we cultivate our inner space for healing, balance, wholeness and beauty, if we do not take personal responsibility for our behavior in the outer world, with respect and even sacrifice, then all our efforts will be for naught. We each have a part to play in The Sacred Hoop of Life.

We must expand our horizons as human beings — the five-fingered tribe — to join with the other beings of the Earth to save what we have, balancing our left-brained scientific and moralistic views and beliefs. Despite our extensive behavior as namers of things in science, the real world operates differently than can be described. Plants and animals exist in a world that is intimately connected with nature and cannot be disassociated from it. Left-brained thinking divorces us from the real world — the really real world that encompasses the spiritual as well as the physical qualities of all things. No plant or animal thinks "I am separate from God" or exists or behaves that way. Every thing upon the Earth, whether human, rock, bird, has Creator's light within it. To reject Creator is to reject self. And not only self, but that which animates, which creates, life itself. From a traditional Native American perspective, by simply thinking in the Western way we kill the world. It becomes lifeless in our eyes, hence, unlamented when life is destroyed, with the rationale: It is separate from us, why should we care?

We are inextricably linked with All That Is and all beings. We must learn to listen, to see, to be. This way of allowing the right brain — the Feminine Power — to come forward is an Eastern way of thought, just as the dominance of the male — rational way — is Western. The Western way, while powerful and good for creating technology, has its limitations in matters of Spirit, and is even worsening with the seeming battle for the soul of the planet between Christianity and Islam. Both are "Western" as both stem from the Judaic tradition. Both are patriarchal, left-brained applications of right-brained activities: talking with Creator. This chasm may seem too great to cross, much less find a way to unite as our world wars along a path of destruction. But all along we have had an open pathway with strong traditions, great insights and incredible power that can unite the disparate ways of thought: Native American spirituality. The late Mad Bear Anderson, an Iroquois medicine man, saw this yearning in the 1970s. And he saw the essential role the American Indian could play in creating a new and better world. He said, "The Eastern religions represent spirituality that looks inward. The Western religions represent spirituality that tends to look outward. We are the people whose spirituality is of the middle. We stand for the sacrality of Nature, for the sacred ways of the Earth. Therefore, we can be mediators between East and West, reminding the others that Nature is holy and full of the Great Spirit."[8]

It is all about learning to hear what is being said to us by the plant and animal nations who share this Earth, learning to see how the invisible world of Spirit pervades our physical world, and being mindful of spirit in all we believe, think and do.

In healing plants and animals, we heal ourselves.

Let's get started.

About This Book

This is the third in a series of books on environmental shamanism, a way of practicing shamanism that unites us with our surroundings and, indeed, all of creation. Each book is a slice of healing, health and wholeness applied to the world. The first book, *Clearing: A Guide to Liberating Energies Trapped in Buildings and Lands* (Findhorn Press, 2006), tells how to energetically clear or consecrate spaces so that they are connected with their highest spiritual expression. The second book, *Finding*

Sanctuary in Nature: Simple Ceremonies in the Native American Tradition for Healing Yourself and Others (Findhorn Press, 2007), outlines ceremonies that can lead to healing, health and wholeness and that unite the individual with the powers of the universe for personal growth and development. This book goes a step further in teaching curative principles that can be applied to our brothers and sisters of the plant and animal kingdoms, and how to learn from them, so that our ailing world is enhanced and enlivened, brought into balance and made whole.

In healing plants and animals, we are essentially healing our world and ourselves, for the world is a circle, all interconnected as One. Only then will we fill the niche that has been provided for us, our own unique place in the Sacred Hoop of Life.

This book discusses not only the hows and whys of plants and animals, but our role as helpers and healers, as citizens of Earth, equally and intrinsically bound with them in this community of nations, with a unique and vital role to play.

We share our world with the plant and animal nations, but we do not really understand them. We have plants around our houses that we love, groves that we enjoy, gardens, even little plants that grace our rooms and desktops, but do we really know them? Do we know who they are, why they are, and what they have to show us? We also share this world with animals we adore: pets who give us joy, animals we appreciate on television, in zoos, in the land and trees around us. But do we know who they are, why they are and what they have to show us? In our modern culture, we do not know or respect these beings who share our world. When they get sick how do we help them? How can we heal that which we do not know?

This book is dedicated to the plants and animals that grace our lives, the beings who share this world with us. It is titled *Healing Plants and Animals from a Distance* because it makes no difference in spiritual healing whether one is near or far. We are always at a distance from plants and animals if we do not understand them, and they are always near and able to be helped and healed, just as they can help and heal us, if we understand them and the nature of true healing, spiritual healing, that transcends all boundaries of time and space.

How to Use This Book

Healing plants and animals is quite simple in theory. It's the actual application, the work, that can be difficult, for it requires that we change our way of looking at the world, understanding the world, our place in the world, and what constitutes our world... and then actively live that change.

There are three principles that make up this simple way of healing:

> Learning to Listen
> Learning to See
> Learning to Be

These principles are woven throughout the book. Together they are the secret to healing plants and animals, near and far, and, indeed, healing Earth and ourselves.

This book provides information about the principles, tools, and techniques necessary to help you harness healing power for plants and animals. It is divided into four chapters: the first being our role in the world as individuals; the second, our relationship with plants and animals and how to listen to and heal them; the third, our spiritual connection with them and how to strengthen it through shamanic journeying; and the fourth, walking in balance between the worlds and in the world, with applications.

Included are instructions and exercises to develop capabilities for communicating with the plant and animal nations, understanding the lessons they have to teach, helping to heal them, and others. Readers are encouraged to keep a notebook of their own observations that might prove useful in discovering new avenues for inner discovery; entries from my own notebook are provided as examples.

The first three chapters of this book conclude with a short review of major points for easy reference, including key search words to find more material about related topics on the Internet. The fourth chapter provides applications and lessons using the principles, tools and techniques revealed in the first three chapters. The book concludes with a glossary of terms specific to doing healing work. In addition, the web site Healing the Earth/Ourselves, at www.blueskywaters.com, offers books, CDs, tools, and additional reading material that may be ordered by mail or e-mail, as well as periodic classes and workshops.

If you absorb the information presented in these pages and practice the techniques described, your inner life and perspective on the world around you will change. You will likely experience healing and peace on many levels as well as the love and joy that comes from giving these gifts to others and Earth.

Chapter One

Healing Principles

The first peace, which is the most important,
is that which comes within the souls of people
when they realize their relationship, their
oneness with the universe and all its powers,
and when they realize that at the center of the
universe dwells the Great Spirit, and that this
center is really everywhere,
it is within each of us.

BLACK ELK
OGLALA SIOUX 1863–1950

The old ones say that the best place to begin is the beginning, and that is a great truth, for when it comes to healing, whether it be plants, animals, or any being, we must first define what we mean by healing. Healing must first be distinguished from curing. If someone has an illness and goes to a doctor, the physician will diagnose the ailment and provide a course of treatment that might include bed rest and drugs to ease the symptoms. After a while, the person is better. But did the doctor cure the disease? Of course not. The doctor looked at the symptoms, compared it with what is known about patterns of symptoms and concluded that the patient was suffering from a certain ailment. Once the diagnosis was made, a set of actions proven to be helpful in alleviating the symptoms was suggested and the patient was left to follow the doctor's orders until the he or she was cured. Again, did the doctor cure the patient?

The patient healed him- or herself. Despite the Western idea that doctors heal or cure patients, no doctor ever heals or cures anyone. A physician may make conditions better for healing, such as cleaning a wound, setting a bone or even performing surgery to remove diseased tissues, but *we all heal ourselves.* The miracle of healing is within each of us, not outside of us. How people heal remains as much a mystery now as it has been throughout human history. We prop up our beliefs in the superiority of modern medicine by assuming that a doctor, or a miracle drug, or some other magic bullet will cure all our ills and that we can transfer our personal responsibility for healing to an outside force: a doctor, a medicine or modern science. But the fact remains that our individual health and that of all beings is intrinsic to the being itself. In shamanic terms, health can be seen as being in balance, ease, or harmony; and "dis-ease" as being out of harmony or out of balance. Our very words carry power as to the state of our ease or dis-ease. We are not shaped by our challenges, but dis-eases are events, actions, or conditions that we confront. This is how shamanic practitioners throughout the ages have viewed health and healing: as a constant struggle between outer forces and inner forces, and the balance, harmony or wholeness of the being. The very essence of peace is an active force and living thing, in that it is a force all around us as well as within us, if only we will see and appreciate it. Peace is the power of balance and harmony as a force.

This is not to say that modern science isn't truly miraculous. People are living healthier and longer and healing more quickly through the astounding advances provided by modern medicine. Even the most ancient practices today are carried on by healers who readily tell those who come to them: Go to a doctor first, and then we'll see what we can do to help in your healing. The role of complementary, alternative medicine is spelled out in its name: complementary, or alongside Western medicine, and alternative, meaning another way that is helpful, not fighting against or contradictory. If I fall out of a tree and break a bone, I want a doctor — and fast — to help set it, prescribe medications to help prevent infection, and perhaps even do surgery if that is necessary for the bones to properly align and hold together. But that doesn't prevent me or anyone suffering from trauma or even chronic disabilities, from seeking aid that goes beyond that which is ironically called traditional medicine. Shamans, medicine men, curers East and West have been practicing medicine for tens of thousands of years, long before Hippocrates. And in their practice they have followed the dictum: Physician, heal thyself. We all are responsible for our own health... our own wholeness, harmony and balance. That responsibility cannot be transferred to a physician or pharmaceutical company. We carry our health, just as we in the Native American way carry our "medicine" — that which makes us who we are — with us all the time, wherever we go. So, how does this — our "medicine" — apply to healing plants and animals?

We Are All One, We Are The World

The physicists tell us that one trillionth of a second after the universe began everything that was and would ever be was the size of a marble. This marble, which could be held in a human hand, though of immeasurable weight, has now expanded to 13.7 billion light years in radius.[1] The universe at its inception was the first Medicine Wheel — a multidimensional circle representing and encompassing everything — and it included everything past, present and future.[2] Just as our bodies are composed of the detritus of stars and galactic clusters, so is the Earth and all beings. If you hold a handful of earth in your hand, you are holding the essential elements of a human body — the only difference being the pattern of energy that holds it together. Our bodies are of the Earthly Mother, as are all bodies of all beings upon Earth; our spirits are of the Heavenly Father, as are all beings; hence, we are Children of Earth and Sky. All beings are our relations. We share 96 percent of our DNA with chimpanzees, 75 percent with dogs, 33 percent with daffodils.[3] When you hold that handful of dirt and gravel — dust unto dust — you are holding all beings upon Earth, all our relations, in potential.

This sharing or overlapping of the genetic materials that are the building blocks of life is a traditional way of looking at the world without the quantification or explanation of DNA. But it includes a broader framework that is, perhaps, less subject to rational review and dissection.

First, as the scientists tell us, we are all relations: bird, tree, rock, flower, dog, human.

Second, we each have a vital place in the great Medicine Wheel of the World, or Sacred Circle of Life, that encompasses everything that is our world.

Third, there is a harmony or stability to the world that is its natural state. This process, when in evidence, is the very definition of healing and wholeness. For example, when a Navajo *(Dine)* medicine man *(hataali)* is called to heal someone, he looks and feels for the harmony *(hozho)* that needs to take place within the person and, conversely, seeks to bring forth what is out of harmony to be seen, understood and either rejected or brought into harmony, for healing *(hozho)* to return. It is a way of bringing dis-ease into ease, harmony, balance or beauty.

When one is in harmony, balance or beauty, one is in harmony, balance and beauty not only within oneself but with the natural — or ideal state — of harmony, balance and beauty of the world. Hence, we are one with the world and all beings; The Medicine Wheel of the World coincides with our own unique Medicine Wheel that is our natural way of being. Since we are connected with all things in many dimensions, just as when the universe began as that marble in the hand of Creator, only now much more spread out, we are in microcosm creating the pattern for the macrocosm, the universe.

Illustrative of this are other scientific discoveries. Among them that electrons may wink in and out of existence, changing from particle to wave and back again, appearing to "jump" from one place to another, and that time itself may not follow orderly rules. One of the most intriguing findings is that when one element of matter is disturbed or changed, an identical particle removed from it is changed as well, even if it is many light years or half a universe away. Forget time or space or unnecessary encumbrances like that. What this means is that if you take a particle from matter and remove it, say, a million miles away, when you poke one particle, both jump. Magic? Maybe. But that is a basic principle of the universe: as indigenous peoples have known for thousands of years, all things are connected. To explain this, scientists theorize that the universe itself may be seen as operating as a hologram. With a hologram, information about each image point is distributed throughout the hologram, so that every piece of the hologram contains information about the entire image. In other words, if we cut a tiny piece of a hologram, that single piece could create an entire, identical hologram. Scientists today believe this may also be the way the brain works in storing information, called "holonomic." We and all we perceive is encompassed within the universal hologram. The Medicine Wheels we create are holonomic pieces, or wheels within wheels, where each piece contains a blueprint of the entirety within it. And as scientists tell us, every piece of "matter" is both linked to and affected by other "matter" elsewhere by subtle energy systems we cannot yet measure but are scientifically demonstrated to exist.

The way of the universe, whether seen by a medicine man or a physicist is the same: all is energy, patterns of energy, whether particle or wave or subtle energy we cannot measure. Thought is energy. Intent is energy. Trees, rocks and grass are energy. Prayer is energy, too. We each are a part of this holographic universe, and what we do affects everything, even if we don't give our actions, thoughts, behaviors much attention. It is all a Great Mystery, as Native Americans often refer to God.

To help penetrate this Great Mystery, we seek the help of powers greater than ourselves, beings of Earth and Sky, powers of the universe, to help us to consecrate the spaces outside of us and within us, and effect harmony, balance, beauty within and all around us.[4] And we may employ ceremonies to connect us with Creator and all beings to aid us in our quest.

Exercise 1 Ceremony of The Medicine Wheel of the Four Directions

A wonderful ceremony for connecting with Creator, The Great Mystery and all the Powers of Earth and Sky is honoring The Medicine Wheel of the Four Directions. It empowers us, connects us with all beings — with the Earthly Mother — and sets the stage for our personal healing and development, as well as connecting with others far away. This may be done at any time, but has great power in the morning, casting cornmeal, corn pollen or grains of tobacco as gifts to the winds in each direction as the sun is rising.

East, opening eyes, being here now. When the sun rises in the morning, it is a promise of a new day. Each day is unlike any other day. It is new. It is a new beginning, a potential, a birth or rebirth into a new world. Each moment is unlike any other, it is new. A Sanskrit poem says it all:

Yesterday is just a memory, tomorrow is just a dream.

The only time that matters is right now.

This "present" is the only present we have. It is a great gift, the most precious gift any one of us is ever given. All the baggage of the past must be dropped for us to truly enjoy and experience this moment. If we are thinking about tomorrow or remembering events of the past, we are not giving our energy to this great Power, nor are we able to receive the great blessing this Power has to give us. This *unoli* (direction, in Cherokee, literally wind), she is red, a primal power. We invite this *unoli* into our circle and partake deeply of her gift. We thank this *unoli* for being here.

South, appreciating vigor, wholeness, healing. When the sun rises to its greatest height we feel the power of it. This is the time of vigor, youth, beauty, greatest strength and healing. Imagine a field of green corn growing beneath the golden sun high in the deep blue sky. The corn creaks as it grows, reaching, reaching, reaching for the golden light, stretching to grasp this golden light, to find fulfilment, wholeness. But its roots run deep in the soil, holding it earthbound, drawing sustenance from the Earthly Mother. We are the corn in the golden light, reaching for Higher Power, healing and wholeness. By giving our energies, our prayers, to this *unoli*, we are given this golden light, this healing and wholeness; we offer our prayers of thanks, our spoken thoughts for others, our gratitude and longings. This *unoli,* she is golden, a light beyond our reach. We invite this *unoli* into our circle, and join with her, feeling her warming influence making us whole. We thank this *unoli* for being here.

West, setting sun, introspection, going within. When the sun sets, the Earth is plunged into darkness; we cannot see our way. We stumble about, blind and unknowing. Sometimes, we know this as The Dark Night of the Soul. Our tendency is to reject this darkness... reject it in ourselves and in others. We go blindly along our way, making mistakes, losing our way, feeling lost and isolated, with questions but without answers, in the void. But this darkness is necessary, vital even, for us, for our world. If we did not have darkness, we could have no light. Creator sees all. Light and dark are one for Creator, but that is invisible to us on this world. Creator created dark and light not so Creator can see, but so we can see. So how do we see? We must see as Creator sees. We look within. We look at the spark of Creator within us to illuminate our way. As we look within, the world outside is illuminated and our path is made clear. We cannot depend on outer things when we are in this direction, The Western Gate. We walk as Creator guides us. This *unoli*, she is black, and comes in many forms. We invite this *unoli* into our circle and join with her, feeling her urging to look within. We thank this *unoli* for being here.

North, cold, white light, Higher Power, ancestors, wisdom. In the darkest night, the stars wheel overhead, shining brightly, as our dreams give landscape to our souls. This is higher wisdom, the white light of truth, the worlds outside our worlds where we come from and where we will go, where the ancestors reside and where the children will come from, the Source of light, of being, infinite. Sometimes the white light of truth is too great for our human eyes to bear; it blinds us, and we erect barriers, put on blinders, to live in denial. We open our hearts, open our minds, bare our souls to this Power, giving ourselves compassion, so that we learn to love and live in truthful, loving ways with all beings, knowing we are one with them, allowing our steps to be guided by those who have gone before and those who are yet to come. We know that what we know, and who we are, is very little. We allow our humility to open us to as much of the truth as we can stand, to help us on our way. This *unoli*, she is blinding white, so we can only see her shadow in this world, a rainbow. We invite this *unoli* into our circle and join with her, allowing her to give us insight, understanding and guidance. We thank this *unoli* for being here.[5]

This ceremony is our Earth Walk here in The Medicine Wheel of the World. It is with us and has been with us since we were born, to be carried with us each day as our steps are prayers upon the Earth, each thought and action a prayer, all leading along a path of Spirit. But we share this world with other beings like ourselves (our relations) and calling all into harmony, balance, beauty is a task that must be done consciously. We become one with the world in this way. But it's not only the physical world that we become one with by inviting in the Powers. We become the bridge between the worlds: blessings from above, blessings from below, for blessings all around. There are four directions plus the above and below directions and the center, that comprise the Medicine Wheel of the World.

We are at the center with Creator.

The Medicine Wheel of the World

In my previous book, *Finding Sanctuary in Nature: Simple Ceremonies in the Native American Tradition for Healing Yourself and Others,* we explored the Medicine Wheel of the World, in which we are the center of the known world and everything derives its meaning from its associations and connections with all things that are brought within this circle. This is the *tonal* — all that can be known, brought within the circle from the *nagual,* all that is and can be.[6] But in this book, we want to establish a more physical and spiritual connection — an intimate connection — with the plant and animal nations. So we will look at our place in the harmony, balance and beauty of the world as the actor who brings balance to the world and our relations. We will turn the Medicine Wheel of the World on its side, so to speak, to illuminate this connection.

Imagine the Medicine Wheel, the circle that is all things within our ability to have consciousness, and imagine that instead of one circle, it is two circles super-imposed. In *Finding Sanctuary* we noted that many indigenous cultures recognize that the Medicine Wheel is a circle that turns both ways: clockwise and counter-clockwise. Ancient cultures recognized this in various dances, such as the Eye of the Raven Dance, where women would dance in one direction, men in the other. This brings Power — higher beings of spiritual power — into the circle. But Creator doesn't see two circles, one of male and one of female, as we do, that is in polarity (up/down, left/right, etc.). Creator has created polarity on this world so that we can see and distinguish between things. So we must learn to see as Creator sees when doing ceremony, healing work or learning to dialogue with plants and animals; we must become one with them, as all things are connected and are not divided or separated. In this circle that is the circle that is the Medicine Wheel of the World, the marble in Creator's hand, everything is connected, even if things appear to go in different directions at once or appear totally separate.

To fully understand our place in Creator's world, in concert with the plant and animal nations, we want to see that power as giving and receiving, as motion and rest, as prayers and manifestation. So, we take these two circles that are one, that are seemingly superimposed one over the other, and we open them to one circle connected with another: something that appears as a figure eight.

The upper circle of the figure 8 turns clockwise, and when it reaches the top of the bottom circle, it continues around counter-clockwise until it reaches the upper circle, where it resumes its clockwise motion, continuing around again, and so on, constantly. Each is a separate direction, but both are connected and flowing one into the other, since in Creator's eyes, they are one. This figure 8 is the formula of Creation — expressed on its side, it is the symbol of infinity. This bringing together to the center, bringing balance to two realms, can be seen as allowing the physical world and the invisible world to coexist in polarity and as one, simultaneously. The person who stands in the middle is the one who sees prayers and manifestation — the shaman, the seer, the mystic, the medicine man or woman. This is the place of power. When we position ourselves here, we become Children of Earth and Sky. We become the nexus of the visible and the invisible, the place where balance is found between the two worlds. We become the one who walks between the worlds.

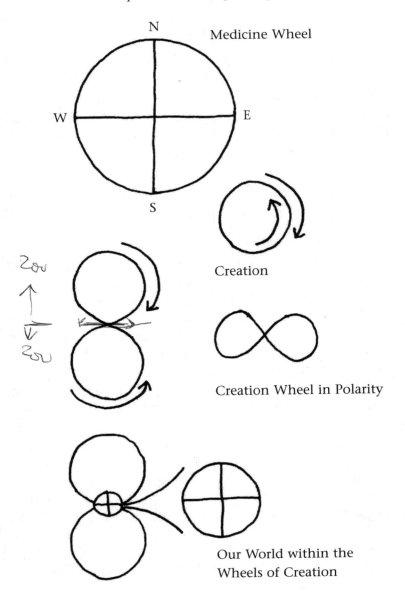

Medicine Wheel

Creation

Creation Wheel in Polarity

Our World within the
Wheels of Creation

The Medicine Wheel of Healing

Throughout time, holy people have instructed us to feel gratitude as a way of touching the divine. This is for a reason. If we are filled with wants and hurts, or solely focused on ourselves, our egos, personalities or material things, then the Flow of Creation is stalled, stuck in personal concerns. When we give from our hearts, the place that is never empty, never knows want and always is full, we make room for miracles in our lives. This is the power of attraction by giving. It seems counterintuitive until we examine our symbol.

In this figure 8 that is our Medicine Wheel of Healing, we allow our hearts to be open to the miracles from above: the Flow of Creation that comes down from the upper right side of the figure 8, to the center. When we have our hearts open, this appreciation of the Flow of Creation coming from above goes down into the invisible world below, grounding us in the physical world (where our feet meet the top of the lower circle), and the energy of our hearts, of our gratitude and appreciation, flows back into the lower world, creating life and blessings of which we can only dream. But the effect is real in the physical world, as well. The Flow of Creation, remember, goes down counter-clockwise into the underworld and makes a complete circle — crossing all the directions, being altered by all the Powers there — before it enters this physical world again. It enters the underworld at our feet, the South Direction — the place of prayers, healing, wholeness, vitality, strength — into what is in the underworld the Northern Gate, the place of Higher Power; continues counter-clockwise through the Western Gate, which is inner light; the Southern Gate, healing; and the Eastern Gate, awakening, before completing the Medicine Wheel at our feet again, entering our physical world as manifestation — literally Creation at our feet!

It continues from this place at our feet, the South Direction (or *unoli*) of the physical, through the Western Gate, and above, through the Northern Gate, where the Highest Powers reside, before it comes to us again at the Eastern Gate, where we greet this Power of awareness in the "now" with gratitude again, so that the process of prayer and manifestation can continue. The movement of the energy forms a Medicine Wheel of Healing that is alive, living in the Flow of Creation, which through our prayers, ceremonies and very beings brings us to be one with Creator.

To view this process of being in the center of this circle, consider the figure 8 as being the universe — all that we can perceive and know and beyond. Where the two circles meet is another circle, a tiny circle that is the Medicine Wheel of the Earth, the physical world, with you at the center. Within this circle is all that you are capable of perceiving in this world — the *tonal*; your connection with the above and below, All That Is, overlaps with the above and below, and you bring in these things of Spirit into this world equal to your own capability (knowledge, appreciation, gratitude and techniques).

In shamanic terms, these three circles are the upper world, the middle world and the lower world. The middle world is the world that we live in daily, our physical world, though when seen in shamanic journey or in altered states of consciousness it appears quite differently. Learning to perceive these worlds and view our physical world through eyes that reveal non-ordinary reality is easily mastered with practice.

To further understand your connection to the upper and lower worlds — or All That Is — consider that marble in the hand of God again. Before the trillionth of a second that created the marble, everything that is and can be, existed in potential. The first thing was a single point that became all dimensions. The single point was a circle that, seen in two dimensions from the side, was a straight line. Thus, the first thing in the hand of God was a circle and a straight line, represented by the traditional medicine wheel, with the circle encompassing all and the straight line going out in all directions which, when delineated to its finest points, actually create the circle, radiating out. Above and below are spirals radiating out, that is, circles in time. These spirals actually go outward and inward at the same time, and in all directions; but for the purposes of discussion and illustration, we'll focus on going above and going below the straight line that is the two-dimensional circle.

If the Medicine Wheel of Creation is seen in polarity, the concentric circle which is two opposite directions at once is turned to become the infinity sign, that when folded on itself becomes parallel lines with energy going above and below at the same time. These spirals of energy, overlapping, become the star tetrahedron, which is the basis of the sacred geometry of the energy body: the energetic form of all things.[7] In shamanic terms again, it is the above force and the below force

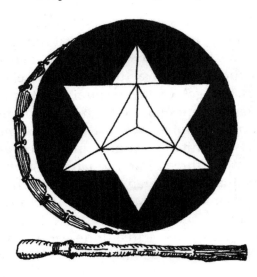

overlapping which creates the living being that exists between the worlds, which is a harmonic between the circles of the above and below, represented as twin spirals. A spiral is a circle in time. Each circle is now, but the spiral connects all the nows in the circle, forever. If time is seen as a spiral of energy, all points in time are discrete yet connected at the same time; past, present and future can be seen as a single point from the vantage of seeing only the circle of time (the spiral on its end, two-dimensionally). So, all time is one time, or now, when all points are seen as one. You can see these ideas illustrated in rock art throughout the Americas; it is a gift of Dreamtime that shamans have shared down through the ages and upon all places on the Earth.

When considering the plant and animal nations, two particularly meaningful concepts of this sacred geometry are the golden mean spiral and the Fibonacci spiral. The Fibonacci spiral is the mathematical formula for all physical forms. It can be seen in a snail's shell and in the pattern in the center of a sunflower as well as a pine cone's rings. The golden mean spiral is the infinite ideal, which in mathematics has no beginning and no end but is a continuous number. When the golden mean spiral — which is infinite — comes into the physical, it translates into a three-dimensional form, which is the Fibonacci spiral. The golden mean spiral can be seen as coming from a plane below this one and expressing itself on this plane in the natural, physical shapes of all things, by using its three-dimensional form, the Fibonacci spiral, then spiraling on to the next plane. (To picture this, consider the physicians' caduceus or two snakes twining, or the DNA spiral going infinitely, but seen only from plane to plane as a segment of reality.) From the Fibonacci spiral, the one (the circle, dot, point, or doorway) is derived from all material forms (the sphere, the dodecahedron, the icosahedron, the octahedron, the hexahedron, and the tetrahedron), which are the basic forms found in nature around us all the time. So, when we do healing with plants and animals we are bringing ourselves and our world into balance and harmony that is expressed through sacred geometry... adapting the ideal to that which we consider real.

The Heart is a Lonely Hunter

These ways of viewing creation, the world and our place in it, vary from culture to culture. My orientation is from the vantage of shamanism in general and Native American at its heart. By their nature, these viewpoints and explanations are resistant to long, expansive, detailed descriptions and explanations. Most shamans view any left-brained knowledge (logical, critical, detailed) as meaningless and fundamentally false. In the shamanic way, left-brained thinking is so limited as to be absurd; akin to holding a yardstick toward the stars and saying "There, I've measured the universe." A person who wishes to be a shaman, or *nagual* (for a *nagual* is both the unknown and the person who perceives the unknown) must stalk his own predilections or quirks of personality or ego that distort and alter a true view of the world and yet not be distracted. Similarly, in traditional Native way, the left-brained method of thinking is seen as The Trickster — coyote or rabbit playing tricks on us, to fool us. If we follow the sly, lying words of the Trickster, it will ultimately lead to our loss and perhaps, our peril. Besides, in this way of thinking it's enough to know that something is so without having to take it apart and put it back together again. Creator creates in a good way to begin with; we are the ones who mess things up. In fact, if we want to truly learn how to be one with our plant and animal relations, we must get into our hearts — or, as some joke, get "out of our minds" — and into the world of right-brain thinking.

Where the left brain (mind) is rational, logical, straight-line thinking, the right brain (associated with the heart) is circular, encompassing, inclusive. These two ways of thinking that Creator gave us are the Medicine Wheel again: straight lines and the circle. Together they form balance and wholeness; one over the other is out of balance. Our world, with its destruction by ego-driven people in mindless pursuit of profit and power is definitely out of balance because of this left-brained type of thinking. The left brain wants immediate, verifiable, pre-judged results, rather than appreciating the total result or all the aspects that go along with an action. The left brain is results-oriented, taking the straightest path to get to a specific destination with anything getting in the way seen as an obstacle; the right brain enjoys the journey from start to finish and all in between is seen as part of and perhaps more important than the destination. The right brain is the realm of vision, insight, compassion, wholeness and healing. But we must acknowledge the left brain and have a logical framework with which to view the world in order to feel comfortable.

Native peoples and shamanism have produced frameworks that work in concert with the hidden or invisible worlds. So we offer this framework as a way of viewing the world that can satisfy the rational mind. Again, we walk between the worlds of the masculine, left-brained, straight-line thinking and the feminine, right-brained, circular thinking. The heart is a lonely hunter in this modern, results oriented world, but if we want to live fully, in harmony and balance, we must acknowledge the needs of our left brain to keep us in balance.

From a right-brained perspective, if all this explanation of sacred geometry and lines of force appears difficult to comprehend, simply acknowledge that we are one with everything: that when we operate from the center of our being or when we are grateful and aligning ourselves with the Flow of Creation, we are a co-creator with Creator, at one with all our relations, including the plant and animal nations.

Exercise 2 Creating God's Marble — Heyoka

In virtually all Native American traditions, there is the concept of backwards way or in Lakota, *heyoka*. In this way, light is dark, forward is backward, yes is no. It's known as being a contrary, such as the *koshares* in Hopi, sacred clowns who dance comically in sacred ceremony.

This is sacred knowledge and a sacred way of looking at the world, because it demonstrates a great truth in a funny way, that Creator created all things as one. It is crazy (Lakota: *witko*) and divine wisdom at the same time. When we perceive an aspect of the world — time, for example — as going one way, we are only fooling ourselves. Creator is All, which means both ways, many ways, all ways. This may seem "crazy," but it is the way of Creator. These very serious, sacred concepts are themselves done *heyoka*, that is, backwards, through laughter. We ultimately laugh at ourselves for thinking we know anything. We know nothing. In the way of the Buddhist mind, our consciousness (personality, ego) that we take so seriously is nothing but "monkey mind," going hither and yon, one moment to the next, thinking if we have a tiny piece of anything, then we know everything. But we do not. We have not even an inkling of the Mind of God. The best we can do is be open to the Mind of God through the Flow of Creation, which propels us forward in The Medicine Wheel of the World. In this way, we become one with the Mind of God, which is always moving, Creator creating.

To see as Creator does, that all is as one, we must open our minds to *heyoka*, to see that all things are only a semblance of themselves. What we can perceive in the physical world is an approximation of what is real, and often wrongly perceived. Time moves backwards and forwards at once; everything moves in a circle, with straight lines providing the force, but with the circle encompassing all. All time is now. We are connected with everything, all the time, all dimensions, all things. We are one with everything.

We can perform a simple exercise that will help illustrate this oneness, and the *heyoka* nature of the world, by creating God's Marble.

Take a small, white ball — a ping pong ball or plastic, practice golf ball — and draw two lines to bisect it north/south so that it is divided into four "slices." Paint each of the slices with a marker pen or paint the four directions as seen from the top: east/red, south/gold, west/black and leaving north white. Hold it in your hand. There, if you look at it from the top is the two-dimensional Medicine Wheel. But the Medicine Wheel is three dimensions in your hand. Hold the Marble of God at eye level. See how the central plane is the Medicine Wheel going out into the horizon, with the above and below. Looking around you, see how you are at the center of that Medicine Wheel. Imagine yourself inside the ball, in the center, holding the ball; perhaps, you inside that ball, in the center, holding the ball... infinitely.

Carry this Marble of God with you. Take it out from time to time to meditate on it. What does it tell you? Can you see the lines of "time" spiraling through the day? Can you see that "time" itself is only how the sunlight falls upon it? Can you see that "time" is actually the shape of the Marble of God, and that all time is within that shape, eternally, everywhere at once? That this Marble of God is not only the physical world upon which we live, but an expression of the universe, where all things are connected? Or see that being in three dimensions and seeing two dimensions is like God being in multiple dimensions while viewing three dimensions — and that, in this, holding the Marble of God, we are God?

By holding the Marble of God in your hands and contemplating it, you are in *heyoka* The Great Mystery (God/Creator) contemplating The Great Mystery (God/Creator) and all things. And, if nothing else, you can use it to play golf, or ping pong. That's *heyoka,* too.

From the Energy Notebook: Touched by the Thunderbird

As a child, I was given to seeing things that weren't there (imaginary friends that really were real), hearing people's thoughts (answering questions before they were asked) and dreaming dreams that actually were the future. This didn't make for a very happy childhood. It usually got me into trouble, and without having anyone around who could understand these things and explain them to me, help me develop the abilities, and put them to good use, it was easier to sublimate them, try to block them out, only notice them when it was important for daily living — even survival, in some cases.

Only one person, a Cherokee medicine man, whom I met in my early 20s, immediately recognized these gifts and urged their development. He tried to teach me, but by then, I was too headstrong (left-brained) and committed to building a career that definitely rejected these qualities. But I listened, understood and used them surreptitiously until life came full circle, and a series of personal crises taught me that I could no longer war against myself, war against Spirit and could not be anything but what Creator made me to be. That is why I was given the name *Nvnehi Awatisgi* (Cherokee for "one who finds the path," or PathFinder, often by going down many wrong ones, so that he may give good counsel), and began following this path of Spirit that Creator laid down. Destiny was unavoidable, and so was acceptance and the obligation of the acceptance of these gifts.

The first bonafide, knock-you-on-your knees vision I ever had was at the age of 17, when I was "touched by the Thunderbird."

One night, as I was laying down to sleep, in the darkness, I saw a small, yellow bird flying around the ceiling. "What is this?" I thought. "Did a bird get in here?" I looked more closely and it looked like a cartoon bird, like "Tweety Bird" in the old Looney Tunes classics, flying in odd circles and figure eights. My eyes followed the circuitous spiraling of the comical, cartoon-like bird until it seemed quite close, filling my vision, and transformed.

What happened next is hard to describe, but the bird turned into the shape of a large bird that was flickering intensely, almost blinding in its brightness. I looked more closely and saw that it was not one bird, but many birds superimposed, shifting shapes so rapidly that they hardly registered on the brain. A voice came from the darkness and said, "This is how people have seen me through the ages." I saw various shapes, from bizarre flying reptiles to multicolored creatures resembling peacocks, shifting rapidly, until for one brief, micro-millisecond, in all its glory, I saw the Thunderbird. Its eyes were lightning, its wings were thunder and the power of its presence shook the universe. I felt as if I had been struck by lightning, paralyzed, and my body "died" for a moment; my mind expanded to encompass the universe, brilliant and intense. I left my body and stayed out there in space a long, long time, ages it seemed, and then, I found myself struggling for breath on the bed in the darkness, waking up, as if I had blacked out. It took me some time before I could even sit up, and when I did, I didn't dare stand, I was too wobbly and weak. But burned into my brain was that image of the Thunderbird. It has never left me.

Among some Native peoples, the Thunderbird is the great power of Creation. Those who see it are instantly struck mad or crazy. Those who honor the Thunderbird in ceremony do everything backwards: *heyoka*. Often, those whom our doctors call crazy today would in ancient times have been said to have been "touched by the Thunderbird."

Those who have been touched by the Thunderbird live out of time. Time, real time, is All Time/No Time. Only in this 3-D world is time linear. In the real world, what's really real, or non-ordinary reality (the realms that shamans see and where healing is done), all time is all the time; everything is all at once, not only in this dimension, but all dimensions.

It is only in the rational mind that those who live in this Dream of The World regulated by clocks (consensus reality), see time as one event following another, like a train upon a track with stops of a, b, c, and so on down the line, going in one direction.

Those who are touched by the Thunderbird cut across all lines of the spiral of time, connecting with disparate events in time: sometimes as glimpses, hunches, insights; sometimes as visions or dreams: or sometimes as extended journeys. As a result, many are committed to mental institutions. It requires grounding oneself, staying present in the now, to "bring back" what is seen, and that is the purpose of this book: to teach the "how" and apply it in healing plants and animals.

The greatest visionaries, mystics, mathematicians and leaders of people touch the Thunderbird — this Power of the Universe — and hold the vision. They are the ones who create the paths for others to follow. From nothing, they create something, because they saw the "something" that no one else could see. They saw something that had never existed, as if it were real, and then brought their vision — that reality — into this reality.

In Cherokee, they saw the path to the immortals (*nvnehi*, in Cherokee, also means "immortals") and with *awatisgi*, the way to the immortals, they were Path Finders (*nvnehi awatisgi*). For most people who have a touch of the Thunderbird, they connect with an event and have the ability to move backwards and forwards through time.

But seeing as the Thunderbird sees (*heyoka*) does not require that one be struck mad; rather, it only requires an appreciation of that way of seeing. It is a way of seeing, a path, that can open the world to one's inspection in a powerful way, and anyone can do it, if they only allow themselves to see that way.

In other words, you don't have to be touched by the Thunderbird as I was in order to be touched by the Thunderbird. That is the power of *heyoka*, too.

Review

Finding balance in the world:

- See The Medicine Wheel of the World, where directions have power.
- Appreciate the right brain and don't be distracted by ego, personality or consensus view of reality.
- See yourself as a medicine wheel, the figure 8, connecting above with below and yourself as the center in this world.
- Appreciate the heyoka, backwards, and backwards and forwards at the same time, seeing things upside down and inside out — and don't forget to laugh!

Internet key words: *tonal, nagual, Toltec teaching, Coyote, Rabbit, trickster, heyoka, koshares, sacred geometry, Fibonacci spiral, meditation techniques*

Chapter Two

Animals and Plants as Helpers

*It's a poor sort of memory that only works
backwards.*

—THE WHITE QUEEN
LEWIS CARROLL'S *THROUGH THE LOOKING GLASS*

The world of plants and animals is shared with us, but it is a very different world, one in which the language must be learned so that a dialogue can ensue. But it is not difficult to learn how to communicate with the plant and animal nations, that ability is part of humankind's birthright. After remembering who we are and how we are in this world, it only requires learning a few techniques. There are two main ways: learning to listen and learning to see. To truly do both really is about respect, understanding how our lives are intrinsically related with the plant and animal nations and the fundamentals of healing. It is a legacy of the past for everyone whose time has come and, indeed, is essential if we are to keep this world that Creator has given us, allowing all of us — human, plant, animal, stone — to survive.

Often among Native Americans the greatest truths are told through stories. When traditional stories are repeated, frequently the teller will say, "The old ones say…" or "The elders would say…" or, "It is said…". The Choctaws, near where I live, do the same thing. They will say, *"Makato, makato, makato, achili…"* which translates into "It was said, and said, and said, and that's why I say it." They mean that the story comes from the old ones, and not from the speaker. It is what was said and is now being reintroduced as an ancient truth, so, we say what is said here.

There are four stories that do well to illustrate how to listen and learn to respect the plant and animal nations. One is Apache, two are Cherokee, one is Lakota. Of course, there are many more, but these are good stories.[1] The first, related in my second book, *Finding Sanctuary in Nature* (Findhorn Press), is an Apache tale about Coyote, the Namer of Things. The story was related in abbreviated form in that book to show how our minds are tricksters. We tell the story more fully here to show some other qualities relating to how and why we share this world with the plant and animal nations. Among the Western Plains tribes, Coyote is a great Power.[2] He is The Trickster, with many stories and legends associated; however, I prefer Rabbit. Among the Cherokee, Rabbit tricks people, too. But he is a bit gentler in his lessons, allowing laughter. Coyote usually has a harsher message; you laugh, but it's the kind of laugh that hurts. *Makato, makato, makato, achili…*

Coyote: The Namer of Things

It seems that one day Coyote was lounging around the house and he told his wife, "Wife, I think I'll go hunting today."

Coyote's wife said, "You lazy lout, what do you mean you want to go off hunting today? You never do anything around here. And you want to go off hunting and be gone days at a time?"

"Ah, but my beautiful wife," said Coyote, "it is important that I go hunting for a few days. And I will bring back some food!"

"Kah!" said Coyote's wife. "Enough. Go then."

So, Coyote trotted off.

After a while, going to the East, and going to the North, and going to the West and going to the South, he felt a strange power come over him. He began naming everything he saw.

(Now here the story gets involved. In the Apache story, Coyote names all the Sacred Plants, how to distinguish them and what they are used for, so it becomes quite lengthy.) Finally Coyote came upon a body of water. From behind a bush by the water a voice came, "Coyote, you have done well."

Coyote jumped back at the voice. "Who are you?"

The voice behind the bush went on uninterrupted, "But soon there will be another who will take your place. This other will be a human being and it will name things and will control the Earth and life will be hard for you."

"Am I going to die?" Coyote asked.

"Life will be very hard under the human beings, especially for you. But, you? No, Coyote will never die.

You were here before them and you will be here after they are gone."

At that point, the voice revealed itself. Out from behind the bush stepped Boy of the Water, an Immortal. And he repeated, "Coyote will never die."

Satisfied, Coyote trotted away to a low hill and paused to look back at Boy of the Water. And to this day, when you see Coyote in this way, sideways, in profile, looking back, he is showing his Sacred Way — his way of showing you he is Sacred. And then he disappeared over the hill.

It is true.

Coyote will never die.

Humans Become Bears

The second story is Cherokee *(Tsalagi)*, about humans becoming bears. *Makato, makato, makato, achili...*

A long time ago, there was a Cherokee Clan called the *Ani-Tsa-gu-hi* and among them was a young boy who preferred to go away all day to stay in the mountains. Over time, he left earlier in the morning and stayed later in the evening, until he would not eat in the home at all. His parents became worried and scolded him, but it did no good. Over time, they noticed hair growing on his body and they asked him, "Why do you stay so long?" He replied that there was plenty of food in the woods and that soon he planned to stay in the woods all the time. Time passed, and he did stay in the woods longer, until finally he told them, "You should join me. There is plenty to eat and you won't have to work for it. I plan to leave for the woods and not come back." The parents discussed it with their Clan, and the Clan held a council and fasted to think it over. Finally, after seven days, the *Ani-Tsa-gu-hi* decided that it was the thing to do to follow the lead of this boy and they left their homes intact, just leaving everything, and followed the boy into the mountains. People of other villages heard of this and sent runners into the woods to try to dissuade them, but it was too late; the people's bodies were already beginning to be covered in long hair. The *Ani-Tsa-gu-hi* told the runners they would not come back, but said, "Forever more, we shall be called *Yonv* (YO-Nah, bears), and when you are hungry, come into the woods and call us and we will come to you and give ourselves to you. You need not be afraid to kill us, for we shall live always."

The Plants And Animals War Against Humans

The third story is Cherokee *(Tsalagi)* about the plant and animal nations deciding to war against the humans. *Makato, makato, makato, achili...* A long time ago, back when humans, plants and animals could speak and understand each other, the plants and animals became increasingly angry at the humans and decided to hold a council to decide what to do about it. The animals were the most aggrieved. "The humans are always shooting us with arrows and killing us," said the animals. "Before long, there will be no more left." Some of the plants grumbled that the humans were stepping on them thoughtlessly, and pulling whole families out of the ground, so that there would be no offspring. As each grievance built upon the other, each animal going round the circle of the council telling of the horrible things humans did, the animals decided they would war upon the humans, and each told how he or she would kill them: with bites, cuts, scratches, poisons and infections. But as the animals became angrier and angrier, the plants decided that maybe they weren't so angry at the humans; after all, humans knew nothing. The plants and animals had taught them how to live, how to feed themselves; if the humans were thoughtless, it was due to ignorance, not malice. They simply hadn't been taught how to live in the right way. So, as each animal, and even some plants, told how they would hurt or kill the humans, some of the plants volunteered cures for each affliction.

As it so happened, there was a young Cherokee couple, a beautiful young man and woman, walking through the woods and they chanced upon this council. They heard everything: all the afflictions the angry plants and animals would inflict, as well as the cures. As the angry plants and animals finished, the young couple ran back to their village and told the people what they had heard. The animals, in hot pursuit to begin the war, heard what the couple said, and surrounded the humans and called upon Creator. "Creator, this is not fair! These people spied on us and heard our plans and now they would use our knowledge against us!"

Back in those days, Creator often walked upon the Earth in human form, admiring what He had wrought and interacting with the humans, plants, animals, rocks and other beings. He appeared in those days as a short, old, bald man with a bulbous nose. He's often depicted in ancient Mayan art that way in art that still survives to this day. He heard the pleas and appeared. "What is wrong my children?" he asked. The angry plants and animals said that the humans' duplicity had robbed them of their powers. The world would be out of balance and a sacrifice should be made; they advised killing all the humans.

Creator thought it over. "It is true that this knowledge could throw the world out of balance," he agreed, "but killing all the humans would be extreme and would unbalance the Earth just as much. Would you be satisfied if the two who committed the offense were punished as an example and a lesson for the people?"

The animals grumbled among themselves, but since Creator was Creator and knew best, they assented. Creator turned to the young Cherokee couple and said, "Are you willing to sacrifice yourselves for the people and bring harmony to the world?" The couple said they would do so, if dying meant peace, balance and harmony could be brought to all the beings. "Then, it shall be so," said Creator, and he gave them a choice: they could be changed into a plant or an animal. "Which shall it be?" he asked.

The couple thought it over and decided that they would choose to be a plant. Creator transformed them on the spot into cedar trees.

And so today, the Cherokee people honor the cedar as an ancestor and a sacred plant that wards off all evil. When sacrificed in fire, the physical manifestation of Creator brings balance and healing to all things.

Star Nations Teach How to Count

The fourth story is one told to me by one of my Lakota teachers at a Native American Church, which honors the peyote plant as sacred sacrament and powerful medicine.[3] We were discussing my sacred pipe (Lakota, *chanupa*) which is called a "star pipe," for if it's held up to the stars, the pattern on it will show from where among the Star Nations it came. This story doesn't specifically relate to plant and animal nations, but human beings, and how they learned to count — the first knowledge. *Makato, makato, makato, achili...*

A long time ago, the people didn't know how to count; in fact, they didn't even know they didn't know how to count. They treated each thing — plant, animal, stone — as individual. There is that plant, there is that animal, there is that stone. Each was an individual and each had its own power, its own medicine, abilities, knowledge, its own being. There was no need to count. Human beings had everything they needed.

But the Star Beings began to visit. First, there were these beings who would point up to an area of the sky and say, "That is where we are from." Then, there were these beings, who would point to a different area of the sky and say, "That is where we are from." After a while, it became confusing. There were these beings and these beings and these beings. So many beings. So, we began to say: one, these; two, these; three, these... and so on, until finally, we learned to count. And that changed the world. Things, beings, became separate things that we could count and were no longer just one, and one, and one, all part of this, which is one.

Stories Give Lessons

Each of these stories gives many lessons regarding the interrelatedness of the human, plant and animal nations.

For the coyote story, one lesson might be that our animal nature is always with us. We share with coyote the ability to name things, which can be tricky, since the named thing becomes a thing outside of itself that may not be its true nature. It also warns that humans are latecomers as far as being the predominant species and with that comes some responsibility. Our status as premier beings may not be permanent.

For the bear story, one lesson might be that we are not that far removed from our animal nature and that we can easily revert; civilization is a tenuous thing, more a belief than a fact of our being. We are related to animals and plants and they are here to help us, if only we ask.

For the war against humans story, we see that the people were taught to respect the plant and animal nations, with the cedar as a reminder that they are related. And that every plant and animal should be treated in a sacred way (not gathering too many at once, gathering in sacred manner, one here, one there) and that there is a cure for every affliction, not only those caused by plants and animals, but healed by plants and animals.[4] Acquiring this knowledge, bringing balance to the Earth, did and does require a sacrifice as well as our acknowledgement of and respect for how we fit in the scheme of things.

For the star nations story, we are reminded that humans and advanced knowledge, such as science and technology, are relatively recent; that we are not far removed from a different form of understanding the world and there is much out there still that we do not understand. And with that knowledge comes loss as well as gain; we learned to separate from the world, to count and measure it, but in separating we lost the sense of oneness. We cannot afford to forget what belongs to us, even if it is out of sight.

The stories in sum also tell us many things. They tell us that once we were closer to the plant and animal nations than we are today and we communicated with them easily; Creator and divine beings were often seen around us and could be summoned at will; and since they are immortal, they are with us still, if we will only seek them, and allow ourselves to see and hear them. The plant and animal nations are still holding to their bargain of providing for us — giving us food, shelter, clothing, medicines, all the things that sustain life.

The stories, in fact, give a view that is common among all cultures: that once humans lived in a Garden of Eden where all things were provided in abundance without asking. But at some point we obtained knowledge. And with knowledge came a separation from plant and animal nations — and divine beings — that today we see as factual. Can we regain the Garden? Well, yes, we can. It has never left us. It is with us still, all around us all the time, complete with animals and plants and divine beings, who communicate with us easily.

As these stories illustrate, the separation between plants and animals and the divine came with a certain type of knowledge; that is, the development of the left brain, in other words, our ability to count, to name, to order the world around us, direct it, use it. Before then, we lived in a garden of unknowing, of being, unselfconscious, just one of many beings upon the Earth with a developed right brain and its ability to envision, comprehend holistically and empathize.

When the cognitive, rational, male-oriented, straight-line thinking of humans became dominant, arising from the underlying reptilian brain of I/me/mine, the world became one of distinctions, of conflict, of building, but also of destroying by separating, by taking the world apart and putting it back together in our own image or way of creation. Since that time, we have seen the rise of civilizations, of agriculture, of nation-states, of war developed beyond all rationality, and of planetary destruction with the touch of a button. We have seen an unbridled impetus for unchecked personal profit without regard to despoiling the natural resources essential for humankind's survival; extravagant rationalizations for wealth amassed in the hands of few; of whole peoples subjugated to want and famine; and entire ways of life, including indigenous spiritual beliefs, wiped out. All products of the left brain. But has the right brain disappeared? No. It's still there, along with its ability to provide compassion — a feminine energy of "womb-like" love; of thinking of the whole, the circle, the encompassing and fulfilling nature; and of conscious connection with others that seeks to find consensus and support.

Transcending Our Left-Brained World

When we focus only upon our left brain, we want everything to fit into orderly niches and for there to be control over things, even ideas. If ideas don't fit into our pre-ordered niches, it causes consternation, even anger and destruction. This will to dominate, order and control, affects what we see, hear and believe. That is our logical, scientific and legalistic way of seeing things — the Western mind.

If we want to access the dialogue of the plant and animal nations, we must bring ourselves into balance. We must create the inner space so that we can hear the outer space in the language in which it speaks. This is not to reject our world or separate us from our left brains. But we want to focus on our right brain, on our ability to be open and vulnerable, to explore the unknown and allow creativity and exploration with an open mind and open heart, knowing that we are supported in this by the world itself. We do this through faith. Faith itself is a right-brained quality that is often only begrudgingly acknowledged by the left brain. We do this by adopting a view of the world that supports us — the Medicine Wheel of the World, the Medicine Wheel of Healing — that allows us to have the rational framework that opens us to a balanced view of objects, beings, relationships, knowledge and perceptions. It is a view outside of the strictures, limiting beliefs, defining orientations and conceptual obligations that are imposed by the left brain (ego/personality) and our Western, logical, confining, restricting left-brained world.

The first step in learning to listen is to develop the capability of suspending left-brained disbelief, allowing whatever chooses to show itself in the moment to come fully into consciousness, and accepting it as so. You become the Medicine Wheel, acknowledging and accepting your left brain, the straight lines from the center, your soul, connecting with the Powers, that radiate out to the circle of all that you perceive and encompass in your world. This is a place of power. The Power is you.

Exercise 3 Finding the Stillpoint

In learning to have dialogue with the plants and animal nations, we must first quiet the internal dialogue within us. Extensively discussed in both *previous books, Finding Sanctuary in Nature and Clearing: A Guide to Liberating Energies Trapped in Buildings and Lands,* a few techniques can help "clear" the mind so that we can hear — truly hear — outside ourselves. This is called finding the Stillpoint. The Stillpoint is the place where one listens. That is, where all internal dialogue is silent, so that your full presence can come forward. Throughout the ages, various spiritual paths have identified the Stillpoint in different ways, but the point always comes back to silence, stillness, being able to hear the still small voice inside that is Creator speaking; that is who we truly are.

The simplest way to find the Stillpoint is to clasp your hands in the prayer position and focus your eyes upon the middle fingers; when a thought appears in your consciousness, simply brush it aside, until internal dialogue is no more.[5]

Exercise 4 Who and Where We Are — Taking Inventory

We think who we are is what we think; but we are not the voices and thoughts that stream through our minds. Who are you? You are the one who listens.[6] To monitor whether you are being your authentic self or simply acting on instructions that may have been accepted in childhood and are no longer appropriate, or are merely being carried around from the past, take an inventory of your thoughts. Look at the clock and set aside 15 minutes. Go about your business, doing whatever it is you need to do, but each time a thought appears or shifts, or words stream through your mind, make a note of them, perhaps using a handheld tape recorder. At the end of 15 minutes, list all the words, thoughts, feelings, judgments that passed through your mind. You will probably be amazed there are so many and you will wonder where some of them came from. From time to time, inventory your thoughts, consciously noting the ones that don't reflect who you really are. Instruct your mind that you don't agree with some of the thoughts, naming them, and suggesting improvements in the form of affirmations, such as: I am a positive person; I believe that Creator gives me all I need at any given moment; I love everyone and hold no judgments, seeing the light within them. And so forth. Over time, your attitudes and perceptions will change, so will your judgments, and, ultimately, your life. If you follow this way of being, the world will begin to reflect the real you, as you perceive what is really you, and you will not be so easily led astray by appearances, by the trickster. Erroneous ideas that have been programmed into your consciousness will fade away as your attention is drawn away from reinforcing them. Your life will change as your perceptions change.

As a second step, take an inventory of your emotions, the same way you did with your thoughts. See where they are taking you, where they come from. Thoughts and emotions are the biggest "drivers" of action, if we allow them to take control of us.

While doing this, you are practicing discernment, probably the most important characteristic of shamanism: knowing where your energy is going. What we attach to — whether thoughts, ideas or objects — defines who we are and where we are... our reality. Unconsciously, we attach to many things; that which we attach to shows up in our words, our thoughts, and is reflected in how we act, think, behave and see. Energetically, these attachments are very real. They are often seen as luminescent cords that actually bring objects, people and events into our lives. We must constantly be aware of our attachments; this type of discernment — which is revealed in each waking moment, and often in Dreamtime, as well — is the hallmark of the shaman.

When we lose sight of our attachments, we become slaves to our thoughts, feelings and events around us, rather than mastering our world, and walking in balance, which requires a measure of detachment. This is not to say we should be uninvolved or apathetic toward the world, ourselves or others just to always be mindful of how our emotions, thoughts and behaviors are expressed, internally and externally. We do not want to give away our power to another, to an event or to any outside force or situation. Rather, we want to be generous when need be and parsimonious when need be, always in the "now." Otherwise, we devolve into mindless crisis and drama and lose ourselves, being defined by external forces and often taking the role of victim. Some people find victimhood, or loss of power, so comforting that they never rise out of it, allowing themselves to be passive/aggressive "snipers" of energy, constantly reacting to events and wasting energy in rearguard actions against the forces around them. These people are never fully empowered, personally, spiritually or emotionally. It is a trap of the mind — Coyote — which should be avoided.

Holding Dialogue with Plants and Animals

As mentioned in Exercise 3, to hold dialogue with plants and animals we must first learn to find the Stillpoint, to quiet the mind, letting all extraneous thoughts disappear so that we may "hear" what plants and animals have to tell us.

You must forget what you know of "language." Human languages are primarily left-brained activities, requiring an array of cognitive abilities including memory and logic. Plants and animals do not have memory and logic. All plants and animals live in the now. A plant or animal does not sit around thinking, "Hmmm, I think that human wronged me yesterday; I vow vengeance and will exact it tomorrow!" So, in order to connect with them, you must also be in the now, in ways that overlap with them.

You have the ability to connect with plants and animals in a way that has meaning and to converse with them, but it is not left-brained, it is right-brained. When we think of speaking with someone, including a plant or animal person, we may think that we are going to speak out loud; and that may be so, if it helps to allow it. But since plants and animals don't think with one-word-before-the-next like a freight train on railroad tracks, but in a circular fashion where all is "now," we would not be able to have a dialogue. This conversation takes place in the realm of intuition and sensitivity, allowing thoughts, ideas, and concepts to come forward. You are attuning yourself to the plant or animal. It is actually a process of "remembering."

This ability is inside you. And it works both ways, a sort of *heyoka* way of remembering. To return to the quote that opened this chapter from Lewis Carroll's White Queen, "It's a poor sort of memory that only works backwards."[7] You must learn, or remember, how to listen inwards and outwards at the same time, allowing the "memory" to come from inside and outside of you simultaneously, becoming "one" with the moment.

Going Back to the Garden

We might call this "going back to the garden," or remembering the Garden of Eden time, when all plants and animals could converse with no problem, before humans developed their left-brain functions.

Imagine the figure 8 again that is you, with the upper loop going to the above place and the lower loop going into the below place, connecting you with Earth and Sky; but also imagine figure 8s on their sides going outward, around you, before you and behind you and from side to side in all directions. The energy of these figure 8s, before, behind, side to side, above and below is cycling at millions of pulses per second, approaching the speed of light, so that they almost become a single pulse, cycling and recycling constantly. This pulse is the principle of resonance, which brings entrainment. Entrainment can be seen in the example of two musician's metronomes. If two metronomes are set at different tempo, they will attune to each other, with the smaller more readily falling into the tempo of the larger. Every human being and every thing in the universe, being made up of patterns of energy, is constantly pulsating. It is motion and rest; spiralling out, spiralling in; and the male principle of direct movement outward, the female principle of magnetism pulling inward, pulsing so quickly that they appear as one. They truly are one, only in polarity in this world. Through this resonance, we send out our personal energetic signature — or status of wholeness in the moment, who we are, where we are, how we are — and it is reflected back to us by everything around us, bringing information about what is there and our relationship to it, all on an unconscious level. This is our connection to this world. We bring in what we need energetically and the beings of Earth and Sky respond, bringing what we need, seeking what they need. It is a source of balance and way of affecting/effecting our world, whether we consciously enlist it to support us to heal and make whole, or not.

The figure 8s — your energy field, your resonance, seeking entrainment with the Earth and all beings — still are within the Medicine Wheel that is you, extending outward, but bounded by your energy body on this plane.

Your Personal Energy Field

The energy field of our energy body extends 27 feet in all directions at all times in this physical plane.[8] We affect everything within this radius without thinking and are affected by anything within this field. You know this to be true. You have often "felt" someone silently walk up behind you within this field, for example, or you have walked up on someone where that person turned suddenly to look at you, feeling your presence. You have certainly felt times when someone troubled or angry came into this circle which reinforces the need for anyone doing this work to learn and practice grounding, centering and shielding. Moreover, everyone has the ability to extend this field of awareness. For example, if you see someone walking down the street 100 yards away and think that you know that person, you focus your intent on that person and he or she, feeling the energy, will turn around and look to see where the energy is coming from. You have also experienced this on occasion, or been the recipient, where suddenly you feel as if someone is watching. Some people go to great pains to draw attention to themselves with clothing, hair and makeup, and actually thrive on this energy, requiring it to feel complete as surely as taking a daily vitamin; without it, feeling in withdrawal, as if something were lacking or missing. This give and take of energy is all around us, all the time, and we all do it to a greater or lesser degree. Some people enjoy the enlivening energy of children while others do not feel complete without giving a great abundance of energy to people, places and things. You also have the ability to deepen your consciousness within this 54-foot diameter, even to other dimensions, to see, hear or feel other places in time and space, often connecting unconsciously with people from the past, present or future. Haven't you thought of someone and wondered what that person was doing, only to have him or her contact you in some way? We are always connected with everything around us, even in other dimensions.

This circle of awareness is the Medicine Wheel of yourself. The circle is all that comes within your awareness, the straight lines go out to connect with all things, and specific things directed by your intent. In shamanism, intent is everything. We want our energy to become inward and outward at the same time, with in going out and out coming in, at once, equally and in balance, and we must do this with an attitude of listening. The way to do this is through connecting with the Stillpoint.

When we open the doors of our perception, we can attune ourselves to the plants and animals and people around us. Since childhood, I have had the ability to read people's thoughts. It wasn't a conscious activity; I had not learned how to open and close the doorways of perception, so the doors would open at odd times. For example, I be walking down the street with a friend and would answer a question, only to find to our mutual embarrassment that no question had been spoken, though it was in the person's mind. This was such a harrowing experience when it happened, mutually so shocking, that as a child I constantly monitored my speech and thoughts and answered people only when I was certain that they had spoken out loud, or simply shut people out and didn't speak. Consequently, I was thought of as shy or withdrawn, or just plain odd. Until I learned shamanism, which answered the questions about these abilities, I just tried to ignore or block or push back down any thoughts, feelings, emotions or perceptions. This was itself debilitating and made not only for a very unhappy and awkward childhood and adolescence, but pops up from time to time as an adult, too, even with training in discernment and perception.[9] I recall that as a teenager I had told a friend, whom we shall call Robert, about this after it happened one time while we were out and about. He told this closely guarded secret to his girlfriend, who confronted me about it at a picnic. "I heard you can read minds," she

63

said, skeptical and laughing about it. I was embarrassed, as it was something I kept to myself, and tried to disavow, and rejected in myself. "Sometimes," I replied, "it's not something I consciously do." But she goaded me, saying I was a liar, which angered me, and then challenged, "I'm going to think something, and you tell me what it is." Upset at the betrayal by my "friend" and at this young woman who was taunting me, and not even knowing if I could do it at will, as I had constantly tried to block out the ability, in no way encouraging it, I said, OK.

So, I sat on the ground and went within. I saw myself in a dark room filled with wires and electronic equipment, and could hear a pulse, or beat, going over and over again: bump, bump, bump-bump... bump, bump, bump-bump... bump, bump, bump-bump... I dug my way through the coils of wires and junk, following the sound, until behind a pile of dusty equipment I found a small television monitor that was the source of the sound, with unrecognizable words scrawling across the screen. I focused on the words until they became legible and without thinking, "read" them — that is, spoke them — aloud, "I love Robert."

I opened my eyes and the young woman's eyes were big as dinner plates. Without a word, she hurried away. Thereafter, she avoided me at every turn, and didn't speak to me for two years — long after my friendship with Robert was over — and then, only to seek help for a problem she was having that she thought my ability might help.[10]

I share this story because we each have this ability. Every human being has the quality of empathy, which is the ability to find emotional resonance with another. Some choose to use it more than others, but it's a quality that all share. Further, it's within each of us to access the "connection" with a specific thing, whether person, animal or plant and derive meaning, either verbal, intuitive or visual. We must only dig through the junk in our minds and find the TV screen, or stereo speakers, or guide or angel or inner "space" that allows it to come forward. Going to the Stillpoint, the void, or empty/full space within is the place to find this connection. Simply practice finding the Stillpoint, then find the inner/outer "space" for this meaning to come through.

Play with it, trying different visualization techniques. Imagine, as I did, digging through the "junk" to find the TV screen, or imagine a special room, for example, full of small monitors, as in the movie *The Matrix*, where different scenes can be viewed and heard. It could be that in your inner space, you are high atop a mountain and can hear the voices below, whatever scenario works for you.

Exercise 5 Grounding, Centering and Shielding

Grounding entails connecting with the earth energetically to ensure that consciousness is not operating from other dimensions or overly affected by other energetic forces. To ground, visualize a thread of energy extending from the base of the spine (the pelvic floor or perineum, the root chakra) deep into the earth, imagining that it connects you to the healing and life-sustaining power of the earth and provides support wherever you go. Do this at intervals throughout the day to reaffirm your established connection, preferably leaning against a rock or tree or something that touches the root chakra and enables you to feel linked to the physicality of the earth to minimize influence from energy forces of other dimensions.

Centering involves locating the core of consciousness in the body and drawing earth energy from below and higher perception from above to operate from a balanced awareness. To center, feel the earth's energy, the life-giving power of nature, coming up through your feet and legs into your midsection. Simultaneously, sense the life-giving energy of the sun — or of the stars at night — through the top of your head (the crown chakra) and into your midsection, where it meets the earth energy coming up from below. Using this process to create a "knowing space" will protect you from upsets and allow you to function in a balanced manner.

Shielding is creating, through intent, a protective energy layer to deflect external negative energy. To shield, visualize a cocoon of mirrors surrounding you facing outward, reflecting unwanted energy. Put on this invisible armor as you would a coat. It can be simply a bubble of white or blue light; it is a shield, but not a veil. It will protect you, but not isolate you from anything. Merely knowing this shield is keeping you safe and that you can summon it to envelop you simply through intention will deflect all negative energy. From time to time, energize the protective quality of the shield by resetting your intention.

Exercise 6 Connecting With Plants and Animals: 'Crazy Eights'

We connect with plants and animals to have dialogue with them by recognizing that they are in the now, and they are also resonating with us if we allow it. When a plant or animal is in your energetic radius, within the Medicine Wheel that is you, it is sharing its energy with you, just as you are sharing your energy with it. This connection is there whether you consciously acknowledge it or not. The word "acknowledge" says it all: to access knowledge. This is what respecting the world around you is all about. When you respect plants and animals from your core of being to and with the plant or animal's core of being, sharing this energy of respect on a deep level, you share knowledge. This is why shamans often reject the term 'shaman' and prefer to call themselves a 'man or woman of knowledge'. It is the knowledge that is important; the way of accessing that knowledge is learned and can be forgotten or unused. One is not a shaman or any thing greater than oneself; it is a term of use, not attainment. That's why shamans don't receive degrees to hang on the wall declaring they are a shaman; one is never an ability, nor does the ability belong to the person, it belongs to everyone and no one. It is either used or it is not, and the knowledge, while retained, is only a tiny portion of what can be accessed; knowledge is in the world, and worlds, including the plant and animal nations.

When you become one with the plants or animals in your Medicine Wheel, the multiple 8s, you are in the here and now with them, overlapping, but also giving to them as you are receiving from them. Consider it a dance or symbiosis; one moves in concert with the other, flowing in awareness, back and forth, giving and taking, motion and rest. Each of you is whole and complete, a system in itself, but overlapping; part of you becomes the plant or animal and part of the plant or animal becomes a part of you. You are, in part, melding, but both you and the plant or animal retain your essential self; it would be again the figure 8, but on its side with the point where they intersect slightly overlapping to share at the point of contact. In this way, it may appear that the thoughts/knowledge of the plant or animal is coming from within you, but it actually is within you and the plant or animal; you are merely accessing the point of common understanding. This is the *heyoka*, remembering forward and backwards, a listening within. Consider yourself tossing a stone of your current perception into the pool of your inner consciousness; by this action, through resonance, the plant or animal that you want to dialogue with will do the same. Where the circles of waves going out from each point intersect and overlap is where you will connect, to be heard from the center of your awareness. You are connected and apart in the *heyoka* way.

Call it "Crazy Eights."

From The Energy Notebook: The Crow and The Oak Tree

As an example of connecting with plants and animals and dialoguing with them, here are two events that occurred while my beautiful wife Annette Waya and I were courting. She lived in Florida and I was there visiting, ostensibly to perform ceremony for an environmental group to help the members find personal connection with the Earth and Powers. I wanted to see the Everglades, and so we traveled to the Mikasuki Reservation and the National Park nearby. As we were driving, I saw that reservation members were offering airboat rides and, never having ridden in an airboat, I said, "Oh, I want to do that!" Annette Waya said it was a tourist thing, surely I didn't want to do that. "Oh, yes!" I said, eager as a child. So we pulled over and bought our tickets. The lady behind the counter said it would be 45 minutes before the next airboat came to take the people out into the Everglades, so we walked along the dock and sat looking at the water. It was a beautiful, summer day with bright, fluffy clouds in a clear blue sky. As we were sitting there, a crow came and sat in the tree above us and started talking. Naturally, I was transfixed by my bride-to-be, oblivious and totally focused on her. But she noticed the crow and said with surprise, "You know, that crow is looking right at you and seems to be saying something." I looked up and sure enough, the crow was leaning down with his head cocked, one eye fixed on me. "You said you could talk to animals," she said, "and understand what they are saying. What is the crow telling you?"

Rather startled, having to pull back from just sitting there admiring her, I looked at the bird and said, "Well, yes, I can probably figure out what he's saying." So I went to my within place. Again, I could hear the pulse of words arising like little bubbles in the darkness. They weren't words so much as little bubbles of consciousness that had to be popped and assembled to find meaning. I turned my attention to them and the bubbles popped with a vision of dark clouds and rain.

I opened my eyes, surprised, as the sun was shining brightly, with only the little puffy clouds in the sky, and said, "He says it's going to rain."

We both looked at the sky and laughed.

We continued to talk and enjoy each other until 45 minutes had elapsed, when we moseyed back over to the admission table. The woman there was talking on a walkie-talkie, and, putting it down, said, "I'm sorry, folks, but there's a thunderstorm brewing and it's too dangerous to take people out."

She gave us back our money and sure enough, an hour later, it was pouring.

Later during this same Florida visit, I was out on the grounds of the place where we were staying and Annette Waya was showing me its various features, flora and fauna and what the owners hoped to accomplish. Their goal was to return the land to its natural condition as it had been extensively farmed; all manner of foreign plants had taken over including some of the plants they were planning to remove. As we were walking, I noticed a beautiful oak tree and remarked upon it, "What a wonderful tree!"

I walked over to the tree. "I need to speak to this one," I said. "It has something to say."

I planted my feet firmly on the earth at the base of the tree, consciously grounding and centering, and placed my hands on each side of the tree. Feeling fully grounded and centered, I went inward to my listening place and sought to remember what the tree was saying. First, it was blank and dark. Then, I could feel my feet like the roots of the tree, going down, down, feeling a cool, fulfilling comfort come from the earth. Then, I was aware of my hands upon the tree; they changed positions slightly, unconsciously, so that my hands felt right, warm. I could feel the tree's rough bark as living but blending with the skin of my palms. Settled, calm, allowing the energies to become one, the darkness of my inner place began to brighten and images formed. First, I saw the blue, blue sky above with fluffy clouds. I could feel my self yearning for that sky, the warmth from above, the energy of the sky coming down, and could feel my hands/limbs/leaves absorbing that golden, life-giving energy. I could feel all the plants and animals all around me as one web of life, each with its own strand connecting to me, and the love of all the beings — plant, earth, stone, animal — as synergistic with the life of the tree... all separate but connected, giving and receiving.

And then, I felt the humans: a darkness of pain and conflict flickered through me like a stuttering black-and-white filmstrip where the individual events were almost too fast to see, but filled with sharp, hurting actions. This filmstrip of rapidly flickering images shuddered my mind/body/spirit and made it yearn for the sunlight, the blue sky, the clouds, the web of life without them. This assault of images almost broke my connection with the tree, but my heart began to expand until my heart energy calmed me and the tree and in that envelope of understanding, we held a wordless dialogue. I gave the tree love and understanding and it gave me the same. It's hard to put into words what we shared/felt as one. But it was an image of healing, of oneness. I felt my consciousness return and lowered my hands; after regaining my composure, my self, I stepped away.

The words came to me as feelings, as if searching for words to tell them. What I told my Annette Waya was this, "All the plants, animals, stones, acknowledge and depend on this tree as integral to this place. It is the grandfather of this place. Without it, this space, this area, this web of life all around, would be out of balance, out of harmony. It anchors, centers and holds this place energetically, so all the beings — seen and unseen, known and unknown — can have a place to be."

This place had been the site of frequent hurricanes making landfall, and after speaking to the tree, I understood why. And I told her, "Because the humans had caused so much pain and destruction to all the beings here, thoughtless, violent acts — physically, emotionally, spiritually — this tree is holding its spirit out to the sky, wishing for hurricanes to blow away the suffering. The plants and animals here, in concert with this tree, are praying with the essence of their very beings for forces of nature to intervene." And I told her, "The owners of this property should befriend this tree, honor it, give it love and respect and welcome its healing power, so that its energy and power is turned toward bringing this place into harmony and balance."

Naturally, the tree did not say these things in words; it took a human being to interpret the words of the tree as holistically expressed. But the knowledge that was transmitted was clear and unequivocal, expressed totally in the now and received by body, mind and spirit.

Perhaps the tree did not have enough power to bring healing and balance to all of South Florida; perhaps only Creator, in concert with all the beings, including humans, can do that. But as far as the circle of this tree's power — the property upon which we were standing — was concerned, it was vital for the healing, health and wholeness of it that those humans who lived there give their energy toward creating a system of harmony and balance with this tree and all its relations.

As I stepped away from the tree, I noticed a bird's nest in the first crook of it, not five feet above where I had been holding the tree's bark. It made me smile.

Annette Waya related what I saw to the people who owned the property, so they might appropriately honor the tree, such as tying prayer flags to its limbs, making tobacco and food offerings for the beings who danced around it and simply sitting beneath the tree and enjoying its shade, the sigh of its branches in the breeze, giving it love and gratitude for its being and the gifts it brings for all beings.

So far, knock on wood, the hurricanes have not returned to this particular piece of property.

For me, I carry the love the tree gave me wherever I go like a little bird's nest tucked away next to my heart.

The Exchange of Energy

We are constantly exchanging energy with plants and animals. For example, once I was driving down the highway with a splitting headache, when I caught movement out of the corner of my eye. A hawk had launched itself from a tree and, as I watched, it swerved so that it was flying alongside the car. I marveled at its coloration, the effortless way it flew so fast, its strength and beauty, and then it curved away. A few moments later, I realized that my headache was gone; and, in its place, I had this beautiful image of the bird, and the internalized perception of strength, purpose and power.

On innumerable occasions, birds have counted coup upon the car, flying toward it, then at the last possible moment before colliding, swerving away, leaving me shaken and energetically shifted. No doubt this has happened to you as well. It is important to note the type of bird or animal that counts coup in this way. Each bird and animal carries its own medicine: the owl walks between the worlds and brings knowledge from the other side; the hawk is a messenger; even the tiny titmouse has its power as a gatherer. Deer, which often collide with cars — thus giving their power to the occupants — are spirit helpers who can heal and provide gentle guidance and protection. Skunks typically are thought of as stinky and to be avoided, but their power is that they are noticed; it means people are noticing you with a powerful impact on their lives. Raccoons can mean playfulness, but also theft, or shape-shifting, a quality you may find helpful in your current situation. Opossums have the ability to play dead, but are tough survivors beyond their seemingly comical way of dealing with the world. How are you being tricked? Or is there an unorthodox or creative strategy that you should adopt? To find the medicine of animals, study the qualities they possess; look on the Internet under totems, or read books about totems.[11]

Those around us, our pets for example, are here to help us and are constantly giving and receiving energy. If a pet is sick, it often is because it has taken on the dis-ease of the human. In this case, healing the pet will have little lasting effect, if the dis-ease of the human companion is chronic or not healed.

The critical issue here is that by practicing inner listening, becoming one with the beings around us and at a distance, and maintaining our own mindfulness, consciously connecting while we are ourselves balanced, calm, whole, we are healing the plants and animals around us, as they are healing and helping us. When we are one within ourselves, we are balancing all the inner elements of ourselves, the physical, emotional, psychological, energetic and spiritual aspects into oneness that affects all around us and brings a greater health to all beings with which we interact. In Tibetan

Buddhism, for example, we are bringing the *la*, the *yee* and the *sem* in balance, harmonizing our *la* or soul, who we really are within, to that which is without, and allowing that which is without to become within. Seen another way, we are shifting our portion of the universal hologram so that the entire hologram reflects a new balance and wholeness from potential into manifestation. Each one of us is central to this bringing of balance to the world with potentially huge effects.

The Butterfly Effect: Unfolding Our Wings

To explain the effect of consciously using your pattern of energy to effect healing upon plants and animals in proximity, and especially at a distance, consider The Butterfly Effect. You may recall the idea that the soft beat of a butterfly's wings in Africa can cause hurricanes in the Americas. The concept originated with Edward Lorenz, a meteorologist and a founder of chaos theory in the 1960s. He was running routine equations in a computer to predict weather conditions and decided to run a series again, only instead of starting from the beginning, to save time, he began in midsequence. To his surprise, the weather prediction was radically different. He rechecked his figures and instead of the number .506127, he had rounded it off to .506. With such an infinitesimal change, the two figures virtually identical, it should have had the same general result. But, since repeated trials proved otherwise, he proved that the slightest difference in initial conditions, beyond human ability to measure, made prediction of past or future outcomes impossible, an idea that violated basic physics. At the time, it created an uproar, but the discovery has since brought about new ways of thinking about the nature of prediction and probability that actually was pioneered nearly a century before by the French mathematician and physicist, Jules Henri Poincaré (1854–1912), who had concluded the same in theory. He theorized that the nature of reality was more accurately described using fractals and phased space — areas of research not "rediscovered" until 1975 and still puzzling to physicists — which also turns modern thought about the universe and reality on its head. He proved the impossibility of measurement by showing that no mechanical or electromagnetic experiment can discriminate between a state of uniform motion and a state of rest. Poincaré obviously was touched by the Thunderbird!

Phased space is how matter appears and disappears and probably explains how one object can affect an object literally a universe away. Fractals are now taught to elementary schoolchildren, reducing Poincaré's complex idea to the simplicity of pictures composed of smaller pictures that each resemble the whole picture. For example, every frond on the fern looks like the whole fern. In fact, his theories could lead to fractals as the key not only for space travel in the future, but time travel — mechanically — since, as fractals show, space and time are one and the same. This also explains spiritually the experiences of shamans and seers for ages. The shaman is at the top of the fractal fern by being at the top of the fractal frond; all realities are only a matter of "seeing," that is, shifting through the octaves of energy that connect one reality or phase of existence to another; or in Poincaré's terms, phasing in space and time.

If all this appears rather out there, consider our heyoka way of seeing the world. Pull God's Marble from your pocket and look at it. Consider if you were a two-dimensional being. Your world would be the flat, a two-dimensional Medicine Wheel as seen from above. But we live in a 3-D world, so we see the marble, understanding two dimensions because we see from three. But suppose you were a four-dimensional being; the world would be an infinitely more rich and complex place. If you were a two-dimensional being and all that you could see, touch, feel and know were two-dimensional things, that is, things that go out and about from you but not above and below, all you could perceive would be two-dimensional. If a three dimensional being appeared in your two-dimensional world, you would see it in two dimensions, as a flat object. But if it appeared before you, went slightly above you and then came in front of you again, say, 50 feet away, it would appear to you as if it had winked in and out of existence. That doesn't mean it stopped existing, it only stopped existing in your world and in your ability to perceive it; it was there all along, but in a dimension than you could not perceive. Called realm shifting, this happens all the time, all around us, but our minds usually shut it out because it doesn't fit within our mental constructs of reality or how things work. When we do catch a glimpse of such a thing, we usually unconsciously dismiss it, or we may even catch ourselves thinking, "Did I see what I thought I saw?" and then the ego/mind kicks in and we decide no, and forget it. Scientists are caught in this dilemma of measuring in three dimensions what we call reality; things which cannot exist in our reality since the basis of science is to record and measure things and make predictions. But as Poincaré demonstrated nearly a century ago, and shamans through the ages have always known, it's a fruitless exercise to try to actually describe reality or what's really real beyond our 3-D senses.

If, in God's Marble, we are living in 3-D and a fourth-dimensional being appeared, we would have no mental framework to make it "real." To make an approximation of a fourth-dimensional shape, one could take a simple one-inch cube and flatten it out to two dimensions; flattened, it would appear as a cross — that is, four one-inch squares down with two one-inch squares on either side of the second square. If each of these squares were then made into cubes, you would have a shape that appeared to be a three-dimensional cross. That would be the shape of a fourth-dimensional one-inch cube.[12] Mathematicians call this a tesseract.[13] In sacred geometry — that is the energy of shapes, or relationships of points in space to create an energy — the tesseract is a hypercube, also called the 8-cell or octachoron. It is frequently noted as the shape of angels, or depicted in art as a divine light. It is composed of 8 cubes with 3 to an edge, hence it has 16 vertices, 32 edges, 24 squares and 8 cubes. In Madeleine L'Engle's classic children's novel, *A Wrinkle in Time*, the young people travel through time and space using tesseracts, although it actually is describing moving through five dimensions.

The key here is understanding that the world is composed of energies beyond human ability to measure.

points create a sacred geometry that allows the Powers (including angels) to enter.

- Umane — From the Lakota (U-ma-nay), meaning "Earth power," this is both a symbol and an act. As a symbol, it is often depicted two ways: as a square with straight lines emanating out (often seen this way in ancient rock glyphs) or as a square with the four points slightly extended. As an act, it is employed in many Native American ceremonies, as uncovering the Earth, and allowing the Earth energy, which is in potential, to fuel the ceremony. Umane could be considered the "sacred fire" of the Earth herself: Earth power. It brings the powers of the universe to bear with the Earth Mother's energy as the operating principle (hence the elongated corners, stretching into space, encircling the globe).

- Antahkarana — This is a powerful and ancient healing and meditation symbol that has been used in Tibet and China for thousands of years. It can effect healing and positive change simply by having it in your presence, enhancing the chakras and aura.

Each of these symbols can be put on the ground or the floor of a room in the center of a circle for ceremony, used as an altar to invite good energies or put under the pillow at night for healing in Dreamtime. The use of symbols creates a morphogenic field encoding the basic pattern of all objects throughout time, and from which all objects may "remember" their archetypal form. It is from this field that angels, goddesses and other light beings may manifest, since their form is encoded within the archetypes of the field.[14] Angles of lines within the sacred geometry of the symbol are used to create doorways for positive energies to enter and aid in healing.[15]

These are not the only symbols that may be used for distance healing, of course, but they are effective, universal symbols.[16] You may copy them from this book or fashion your own, and they are available from other sources.[17]

The Spirit Form of Plants and Animals

We are each energetic systems, taking in and expending energy as self-contained units within an environment that sustains us. Our unique pattern of energy determines who and what we are: plant, animal, human, stone. If we only look at the physical we see the outward form, which is itself only the densest part of the energy body. Our true energy body encompasses the physical and beyond. In our spirit form, we are beings of light, with areas of darkness that need healing. This is how plants and animals heal us: they provide the light, or energy, to allow us to shine more brightly, in better balance. And we provide light, or energy, to heal plants and animals, if we direct our energy to do it. That is, if we are connected with our life-giving, healing energy through intent. In this, we are at once powerful co-creators with Creator, able to consciously direct energy through intent, and the weakest of the weak, in our ability to easily disconnect with the forces of nature all around us, living solely upon intellect.

We must use both sides of our brains — the right for drawing in all the knowledge holistically, the left for sorting it, making sense of it, if we are to consciously dialogue with plants and animals and heal them. In the energy notebook section on The Oak Tree and The Crow, how did the crow know it was going to rain? How did the tree know how to attract hurricanes? Because they are both totally in the here and now, as are all plants and animals. All energy medicine takes place in the here and now. With our left brains, we connect dots or points in time with intent; but with our right brains, we are able to connect all the dots, even the ones that don't seem to make sense, tapping the underlying reality that is within each moment. Real time, as best we can experience it, as opposed to clock time, is a "V." Our left brains only perceive the top planes of the V, filling the chasm from point to point to achieve a desired goal, following our intent. But if our intent is to go as deeply as we can within the moment, then we spiral down between the top planes of the V, as deeply as we are able to exist within the moment, each moment, so that our consciousness is going deeper to go higher. That is, *heyoka* again, by going more deeply into the moment, we are also raising our vibration rate, a subject that will be discussed in more detail later. Since plants and animals are always deeply into the moment, totally present, when we connect with plants and animals energetically, we are using our power to assist them, just as they are assisting us. They are assisting and joining with our right brain functioning, and through our left brains, our organizational skill, we are being co-creators with Creator, if our intent is good, that is, going with the Flow of Creation.

The crow was able to tell the future because it was touching All Time/No Time. It didn't consciously say it was going to rain, but could feel it, sense it, see it as a potential with great probability. My thoughts were about riding the airboat — that was my intent — but the crow could see that was not going to happen and my intent was unfruitful; it had low potential, low probability. It was noticing the conflict and "saying" that my intent was askew, that the reality of the future was different. By connecting with my right brain, my left brain was able to sort through the information being given by the crow so that it made sense to my situation: it was going to rain.

Someone truly adept could actually see through the eyes of the crow, and not only see the rain in the future, but other things, as well, that would harmonize or conflict with intent (an ability that is more easily offered through shamanic journey and in Dreamtime). This ability can be developed over time, with practice, but it requires persistence.

The oak tree was able to call the hurricanes because it was connected to all within its circle: birds, rocks, animals, other plants. Hurricanes might come, regardless, because of the Earth energy of the place and where it is situated near the ocean; but that precise spot as landfall had greater probability because the plants and animals, in concert, created a greater potential for it to occur there through their intent. When animals suffer, they shed energy by shivering and shaking to draw energy to the areas of pain, shucking it off, as a form of healing release. When plants suffer, they, too, release energy, even dying to release the toxins around them physically, spiritually, energetically. They also draw in energy, whatever the plant or animal knows and has power over to help it heal. The plants and animals in this place, knowing that hurricanes — great winds and rain — cleanse, purify and start cycles anew, were releasing their pain by drawing in the conditions for hurricanes to land there.

Spirit 'Blueprint' Is Encoded in the Plant or Animal

All plants and animals have within them the blueprint of how they should be. They carry it with them, as do we. Scientists call it DNA: the codes with the specific patterns of energy that will replicate themselves from one generation to the next. If damaged, they will restore to wholeness or provide the way for wholeness for future generations through evolving to meet existing or shifting conditions. DNA, the patterns of energy that define physical presence, is not set in stone. It can be shifted as conditions require. Even if the individual plant or animal is disfigured, the pattern of its energy — its spirit body — remains.

This spirit body of plants and animals has also been observed by scientists. In the 1940s, Dr. Harold S. Burr at Yale University, measuring electrical conductivity, mapped the energy fields around living plants and animals.[18] He found that a salamander has around it an energy field in the shape of an adult salamander; but, surprisingly, he also found that even the unfertilized egg of a salamander had an energy field roughly the shape of the adult salamander. Also, in the 1940s, a Russian researcher, Semyon Kirlian, discovered that when a portion of a leaf is cut off, the remaining leaf has an energy field that continues to show the whole, uncut leaf. He called this The Phantom Leaf Effect. Refining the measurement techniques, Ion Dumitrescu in Romania found that the energy field was so precise as to even include the intricate patterns of the veins on the back side of the missing leaf part. Burr also found that plants react to the movements of the sun, moon, tides and planets, showing they are intimately connected to and aware of their environment beyond the ability of humans.

Then in 1966, an FBI polygraph expert and trainer, Cleve Backster, using adapted polygraphs, found that not only do plants react to physical events around them, but he documented changes in leaf conductivity when the plants were threatened with injurious thoughts and showed they responded to angry emotions or disturbances outside of their physical presence. They even reacted to positive events such as receiving water before the water was poured. He documented that plants react with what can only be described as feelings, and can accurately assess the thoughts of those within and outside of their energy field.[19] Since then, with over 35 years of meticulous research, Backster has undermined conventional science's portrayal of a universe comprised of discrete entities by meticulously documenting the intricate web of sentience among all beings, even those we don't normally associate with consciousness.[20]

Today, doctors and hospitals routinely use electronic scanning devices, such as EKGs, EEGs and MRIs to scan the physical body and measure its electrical outputs creating an energetic map that can determine dis-ease.

But other than understanding how to design and build the machines, they don't know how or why scanning human energy fields works. The scientists are mapping the spirit body, but in a very limited, mechanical fashion. Healers and shamans have been doing this for thousands of years.

The critical missing factor in this science, is spirit. When the spirit body is reduced to merely being acknowledged, however grudgingly, as a physical manifestation, it loses its infinite power to transform. Scientists can map the electrical output of a plant or animal with their left brains, but it takes the right brain to make the connection that all things are connected. The animus or life force is the connector, and physical manifestation — the visible — is an outgrowth of the invisible: the divine. Science has the power to transform matter. Spirit has the Power to transform anything. Science is limited to observable, visible phenomena in the physical world. Invisible Spirit creates the physical world. The trick, so to speak, is to allow ourselves to be in the center of the Medicine Wheel, between the straight lines of intent and the circle of Spirit, to effect healing.

Exercise 7 Seeing the Spirit Form of the Plant or Animal

A simple exercise for seeing the spirit form of the plant or animal we want to treat is to simply look at the plant or animal very closely and imprint its physical appearance — complete with areas to be treated — in our mind. This can be done either in proximity or at a distance through a photograph. Set aside about 30 minutes for this. Carefully study the plant or animal, noticing every detail. Then go to another room or space where you feel comfortable to meditate and allow your mind to open, reaching the Stillpoint. Meditate, drum or rattle, whatever way helps you to reach the Stillpoint, and observe what you feel about this plant or animal. Don't dissect or analyze the impressions, just allow them to come to the surface of the mind holistically. Allow and accept each bubble of thought, whether in words, visions, impressions, shapes, feelings, and gently release them. After you have come back into normal awareness, take pen and paper and draw the energies of the plant or animal. Feel free to express whatever is retained from the All Time/No Time of the meditation.

The drawing does not need to actually resemble the physical shape of the plant or animal. For example, it could be the general shape of the dog, but with one ear grossly out of proportion with energy radiating out from it, perhaps in violent colors. Even if the hurt portion is the foot, the portion to be treated may actually be the ear, as shown to you in your meditation. In energy medicine, the afflicted area may be where the energy is coming out in the form of dis-ease, not the source of the imbalance. It could be that in the drawing of your meditation, a point is shown to you that is a trigger point, perhaps unrelated to either the source or the exit wound, but a specific place that needs healing that will balance both. The treatment itself will be shown to you: it could require healing with the hands or simple prayer. It could be that an image or symbol of wholeness will be shown to you and that merely focusing on the symbol in prayer will bring balance to the plant or animal. Or, it could be that a symbol of the whole plant or animal will be shown to you in spirit form, as the plant or animal should be as a whole, complete and healthy being, that will serve as your guide for prayer. Trust in Creator and your connection with Creator, the divine within you that connects with all beings, will show you the way.

Connecting With Divine Beings, the Powers: 'We Are What We Think'

Divine Beings exist beyond all boundaries of material time and space. Materialists believe that only physical manifestation is real; but what is real comes from belief. If, for example, we believe the world is flat, then the world is flat according to our belief system and everything we see will conform to that belief. If you doubt it, see Galileo. As Buddha said, "We are what we think. All that we are arises with our thoughts. With our thoughts, we make our world."

When the Europeans' first ship appeared on the shores of the Americas, the indigenous peoples literally didn't see them. There was nothing in their belief system to support such apparitions. They appeared as birds and waves upon the water. It is said that shamans were able to point the ships out to the people because they were used to seeing patterns that did not fit ordinary reality, in this case, the way the clouds (billowing sails) and waves (wooden bow) met to form a new thing. Only then were the people able to see the ships.

Only when we allow our minds to accept the shapes that appear before us will our world be peopled with the divine beings that constantly walk among us.

All cultures have divine beings. It has been said in recent years that Native Americans did not believe in goddesses, angels or divine beings; they say this to distance themselves from what is derisively termed New Age thought. If this is so, then what was the White Shell Woman of the Navajo Creation Story, or her sister, Changing Woman? Who are the kachinas of the Hopi? Who are the *adawi* of the Cherokee, or Ixtel, the divine being that the Mayans still honor? Who are the Powers that medicine men supplicate to help them create miracles? The divine beings of the world have different faces that appear to different cultures, but they are similar and the same by whatever name is given to them. When the Cherokee medicine man asks the Blue Deer and the White Deer and the Red Deer and the Black Deer to come to his aid in curing a person, he is calling to the divine powers of these spirit animals.[21]

As is more fully outlined in my previous book, *Clearing*, our world is populated by divine beings of all stripe and caliber. Some goddesses are connected to a particular place, such as a sacred site, a mountain or a valley, while others manifest in many places simultaneously and are timeless enough to exist in the past, present, and future. Goddesses can be seen in the flames and smoke as visions, often small but sometimes rising to great heights. People have experienced such fire visions for thousands of years.

Other beings include elementals, variously known as sprites, fairies and elves. Many of these beings, especially elementals, attend to the Earth's energies and manifestations such as plants and water, and every culture has a name for them: faeries in the British Isles, little people among the Cherokee, *dryads* in Greece, *leshiye* in Russia, *shedim* among Jewish people, *afries* in Egypt and *yowahoos* in Africa. Some are quite powerful. In Ireland, for example, there are the powerful Tuatha De Danaan, subjects of the Celtic goddess Danu. Although lumped under the category of fairies or elves, they are believed to be descendants of star beings who populated the earth ages ago and are, maybe not so coincidentally, similar in power and history to the beings ancient Tibetans described as the Lha. The Lha, according to a thirteenth-century account called the *Chojung*, came to earth when it was devoid of vegetation and manifested plants and animals through a form of deep meditation called *samten se*, which they eventually forgot how to do. Even elves, who are portrayed almost comically in popular culture, have a more powerful pedigree. The name derives from the Scandinavian *alfar*, referring to spirits of the mountains, forests and waters. Elementals have a range of energetic qualities. Some entities with positive energy are beneficial, such as those inhabiting plants and trees. Others with negative energy appear in nightmarish contexts, such as the creatures seen by alcoholics having delirium tremens. Our world abounds with beings positive and negative that largely go unseen; we are like fish in an ocean that refuse to see other fish.

It is important to note that negative emotions attract negative entities that feed on them, while positive emotions attract positive entities. That is why in any shamanic practice one must avoid succumbing to fear, which feeds negative entities, making them appear more terrifying and powerful. In fact, most negative entities are harmless but know how to create a fearsome appearance. The way to defeat a fear-provoking entity is by generating love or laughter. Positive energy is painful and repulsive to negative entities and will cause them to scatter, while at the same time attracting positive entities.[22]

As noted in Chapter One, we can enhance our ability to heal plants and animals by appealing to the Powers, such as the *unoli* (the directions). But we can also appeal to those who inhabit the land where we are working, or where the plant or animal resides. All it takes is intent and supplication. Simply ask and be grateful. We offer prayers to thank the divine beings for their help before they appear so that they do appear. If we offer a prayer that says, for example, "Please come to our aid," that allows for not coming to our aid. When offered as an affirmation, as in "Thank you for your help," we are supporting the act as a process already in motion and having already taken effect even while the physical action is promoting an effect.[23] It may seem *heyoka* again, but we ask for help by thanking for help given, acknowledging the reality before the reality occurs, because it has already occurred when we ask. We allow, accept, acknowledge and are grateful. Divine beings operate in All Time/No Time, so their intervention is assured, if we allow it. We allow it through prayer, expectation and intent.

To do healing work on plants and animals in proximity or at a distance, it is useful to create a space for miracles, allowing divine power in. This is defined both in physical space as well as in Spirit space, in the inner world and the outer world. For the outer world, you can define a circle using corn meal or tobacco and sitting within it.[24] We give a prayer thanking Creator and all Divine Beings for allowing us to be in this space, inviting them in and thanking them for acting as doorkeepers, keeping all negative energies out. For the inner space, we remember that we are divine, too, that we are co-creators with Creator and have the spark of Creator, the good medicine, *nvwati*, within us. This can be understood in the Sanskrit greeting, *Namaste*, which literally means, "The divinity within me greets the divinity within you." We should remember that we are all divine beings in human bodies, and that we share and are connected with every other being — human, rock, plant, animal — on this, our Earthly Mother.

We Are What We Feel

Before we attempt to heal plants and animals, we must acknowledge not only our thoughts, but also our emotions. All matter, even thoughts, have vibrational frequencies — some are high, some low. We intuitively know that when we are closest to Creator, to the divine, our vibration rate is at its highest. But until David R. Hawkins measured the vibration rates of emotions, there was no scientific evidence for this.[25]

Over 20 years, Hawkins conducted experiments using kinesiology, or muscle testing, which demonstrated the human body becomes stronger or weaker depending on a person's mental state. He developed a scale of 1–1,000 that maps human consciousness: 200 (or 20,000 cycles per second) weakens the body and from 200 to 1,000 makes the body stronger. Specifically, he measured rates for emotions such as: shame, 20; guilt, 30; apathy, 50;

grief, 75; fear, 100; desire, 125; anger, 150; pride, 175; and courage, 200.

Anything below 200 is destructive to life for both the individual and society at large; all levels above 200 are constructive expressions of power. The divine or enlightenment levels are in the 750–1,000 range. Above 200 are: neutrality, 250; willingness, 310; acceptance, 350; reason, 400; love, 500; joy, 540; and peace, 600.

Sadly, Hawkins concluded that 85 percent of the human race calibrates below the critical level of 200, while the overall average level of human consciousness was approximately 207.

It's perfectly understandable that emotions are capable of a higher vibration rate than thoughts, if you have ever noticed that emotions frequently are impossible to describe in words, or clumsily at best, since they are laden with a wealth of ideas and perceptions beyond the left brain's ability to process. That's because the mind can only process information at 1/30th of a second. That's measurable. If you look at the effects of a strobe light, as long as the interval between flashes is slower than 1/30th of a second, it appears as if moving things are "frozen" in time. If the strobe flashes faster than 1/30th of a second, moving objects appear to be moving fluidly because the mind fills in the gaps. This is known as persistence of vision, and it is the reason we are able to "see" motion pictures as fluid, rather than many flashing frames. It appears "normal" even if the light is still flickering because we don't "see" gaps that are quicker than 1/30th of a second with our conscious minds. That's also how subliminal messages are sent: on the borderline between conscious and subconscious perception. Thinking occurs at the speed of reading; you "think" as fast as words form and are processed. But consciousness is at the speed of light. Hence, to access higher consciousness, emotions form a bridge with the higher emotions blending with the lower levels of higher consciousness itself. The right brain exists within this shadow world of emotion and symbolism that connects with higher consciousness. Mystics throughout the ages have accessed this for wisdom, and healers touch through the Stillpoint to bring higher energy into manifestation. While the left brain is plodding along trying to make sense of its surroundings and place in the world, the right brain is holistically and immediately conscious of everything that it can process at that moment, at the speed of light itself.

Plants and animals, not slowed down by words, logic, rationalizations and time sense, are closer to universal mind than are humans, but lack the sophisticated organizational ability of humans. It is up to us as co-creators with Creator to bring the unlimited scope of universal mind, accessed by the right brain, into balance with the left brain's ability to sort and process information and, through ritual, ceremony and intent, manifest outcomes.

You can determine your own consciousness level through kinesiology. Clear your mind, accessing the Stillpoint, and place your right hand palm down over your solar plexus and ask a simple yes/no question. See which way your hand seems to inadvertently move. It could only be a hint of movement, more an indication than an outright jerk or steady movement. For example, state your name clearly and see which way your hand moves or inclines to move. If "yes" is having your hand move inadvertently left and "no" is having it move right, then you can ask, "Is my vibration rate 200?" If it's yes, then ask, "Is it 300?" and so on until your hand moves the other way. This is a way of connecting with the inherent wisdom of the body. Your body, like that of plants and animals, is connected to the now. Note that when using this technique, you should calibrate yourself, so to speak, each time you begin. Ask obvious questions at first to determine which is "yes" and which is "no." If your mind is clear, in the present, in the now, you can assess your vibration rate, and much more.[26] Practice using your hand with yes/no to check your vibration rate.

Before doing energy work, it's imperative that we raise our vibration rate as high as possible. Once the healing ceremony is under way, our vibration rate will increase as the ceremony progresses. But unless we can attain the tipping point when starting the process, our efforts will fail. How to do this? Motivational speaker and author Wayne Dyer uses a wonderful image to describe connecting with the divine and its energies: Imagine riding a streetcar with hanging straps above to hold on to when the going gets rough. No matter where you go in life, those straps — Divine Will, the power of Creator's will for your life, the Flow of Creation, our Higher Power — are always within reach. Just imagine reaching for the strap and hanging on.

Another analogy he uses is to consider how you are focusing on your world and everything around you. The first person who discovered that a ship could be made of steel or that an airplane could fly, he notes, was not looking at the heaviness of the objects, but their buoyancy. Who could have imagined that ships the size of small cities could float effortlessly upon the seas, or that craft weighing thousands of tons and carrying hundreds of people could fly through the air? The water and the air were and are the same now as then. We are the ones who view our world with pessimism, skepticism and certainty over what will happen, or with hope and possibility that anything can happen.[27] Skeptics will always find reasons for skepticism, and angry people find themselves living in an angry world filled with angry people, but people of hope and certainty of faith often prove the impossible and accept it as the way of the world. Opening your heart is the key to performing miracles.

Before doing healing work, think loving thoughts. Revel in them! Savor them. For me, there are certain memories that trigger heart opening; for example, I recall my son when he was about three years old dancing in a sunbeam. I was in the den and heard a noise in the kitchen. Peering in, I saw him, bathed in sunlight, dancing in delight at the sun's rays. Such pure joy, such bliss. The memory never fails to elicit a smile, a touch of the miracle of youth. But this can be done in other ways, by simply affirming love for all beings, imagining beings of light or delighting in the senses.

Hold your right hand to your solar plexus and affirm: Dearly Beloved, I give my heart to thee (or a similar mantra that expresses love). This works also whenever dark thoughts enter our consciousness or negative self-talk circles in our heads.

Take a deep breath, exhale, breathe again, and affirm: Creator, thank you for all things; thank you for this moment; thank you, Earthly Mother, for all the abundance you provide. Allow, accept, acknowledge and be grateful.

That is the doorway to the heart. We begin each ceremony with prayers of gratitude and affirmations of love to raise the frequency of our thoughts, suffusing our energetic matrix with adaptive, divine, creative power.

Four Ways of Using Energy

There are four basic ways a person can heal using energy medicine: channeling, reflecting, taking on and melding.

Channeling allows a divine being, or beings, to use the body as a hollow bone for healing. This may be done through enlisting the Powers of Earth and Sky, or through Reiki, the Eastern practice of hands-on healing, that allows the Reiki guides to send healing energy to the person, plant or animal.[28]

Reflecting is using your energy field to reflect back to the person, plant or animal what is missing or out of balance with the one being treated.[29]

Taking on is a rather difficult and potentially very dangerous method whereby the dis-ease is taken on by the healing practitioner and healed. For example, one of my activities is doing the Bear Dance, a spiritual practice like Sundance, whereby the dancers take on the illnesses of the people in attendance and all beings to some extent, by dancing the Bear. Through ceremony, we become the Bear, the spirit of Bear, and so it's the Power of the Bear that heals. The dancers themselves practice clearing and cleansing techniques upon themselves, primarily *Inipi/Asi* (sweat lodge) for purification, before and after the dance. During the dance, the dancers are constantly bathed in sage smoke to keep them in spirit and prevent the dis-eases from attaching to them while the Bear Spirit transmutes the dis-eases. Taking on should only be done after, and with, intense spiritual training and experience.

Melding (or blending) is becoming one with the person, plant or animal being treated, so that dis-eases may be removed. This is not advised with human beings, but it can work well with plants and animals, if one is firmly grounded, centered and shielded.

In all of this work, you must be careful in how you use energy. It is important that you are discerning in your use of energy, using personal energy only rarely, relying instead on the energy of the Earth or the Powers to effect ceremony or perform healing. When I first started out in healing work and in ceremony, I mistakenly believed that the harder I prayed or the harder I tried or the harder I did something, the more powerful that prayer or ceremony might be. In fact, the harder we work, the less effective we often are because our own exertions and depletion of personal energy gets in the way. Our sources of energy in daily life are rest and sleep fueled by the power of dreams; energy from the plants and animals we consume; energy from the air we breathe and the water we drink, gifted by the Earthly Mother; and the gifts of the Divine all around us, if we ask and are able to receive. A good rule of thumb is to focus your intent and allow Creator and the Powers to do the work, using perhaps 10 percent personal energy and 90 percent Creator and the Powers. I say 10 percent only to focus the mind and stress that some personal energy is required to stay present, when in fact Creator and the Powers really do all the work. We must walk in balance, in beauty, to stay refreshed and whole. Personal energy is finite; divine energy is infinite and Earth energy virtually so.

Consider it this way: if energy were measured in dollars, each day a certain allowance is deposited into your daily account. That amount is spent in various ways, from simply being conscious, to using muscles, to any type of energy medicine. If you go over the limit, you are drawing from reserves and are depleted, tired, run down. Energy medicine requires enormous amounts of energy; but it is energy that is "run through" the body, not personal energy draining the body. If you become tired doing energy work, it means you are depleting your personal energy. Allow Earth energy to pass through you, or reflect what is around you, depending on the circumstances. Even with prayer, one expends only a relatively small amount of energy, just enough to provide guidance and structure while allowing Power to come through. Creator does the work. It doesn't do any good or make the effect any better, to pray "harder." Pray better, not harder; direct your intent toward achieving the ceremony, allowing miracles to happen. Creator creates the miracles.

There is yet a fifth way of using energy: healing with the whole being. We may approach this through conscious intent, but we haven't mastered it yet. Great souls such as Jesus and Buddha showed us the way. This is the universal healing power that transcends common human achievement. Indeed, through perfecting our discernment, intent and healing abilities through seeking harmony, balance and wholeness, we are following in that path. The time is now, with Earth in crisis, for each of us to redouble our efforts toward bringing healing, health and wholeness. But there is a caveat: consciously applying the whole person to healing can often bring unhealed portions to the surface in anyone you come into contact with, throwing people into turmoil because they cannot handle these errant pieces of themselves. The story of Jesus, for example, is as much how to live the right way as it is an example of how His perfection brought out the unhealed portions of others and society. Crucifixion being the only way the culture then — and often now — can deal with unhealed portions of ourselves coming forward. Just as a bright light causes darkness to disappear, so the brighter light exemplifies that darkness can be as deep, and that light in addition to illuminating also reveals flaws that might otherwise have gone unnoticed.

Of the four ways, we meld every time we hold dialogue with plants and animals. That in itself has a therapeutic effect, for it shows us ways we can help bring the plant or animal into wholeness or balance. Reflecting is something we also do all the time, whether we are aware of it or not. When you and your best friend, for example, have a mutual friend whom one of you loves and the other dislikes, that is an example of reflecting. Something about the person resonates with one and repels the other. One may feel happy, refreshed, enlivened and creative in this person's presence, while the other has nothing in common and may even seem to disagree with everything this person says. We each are mirrors of each other. A person may reflect unhealed portions of oneself that are seen as repugnant, or a person may reflect areas that seem to bring out the best.

When we perform the exercise of creating a Medicine Wheel, a prayer or meditation space for healing, we are actually focusing our mirrors, so to speak, so that the plant or animal has reflected to it the energy it needs to heal or be made whole. Even at a distance, by seeing itself in what is reflected by you, it can allow its inherent wisdom to take over and make itself whole.

When doing the exercise of drawing the energy of the plant or animal and focusing on what is whole and complete, as opposed to what is out of balance, we are reflecting to the plant or animal what is lacking. The same is true when we practice raising a plant or animal's vibration rate. Both allow the plant or animal to reflect against its own "blueprint" so that healing can occur.

As for channeling, the act of inviting the Powers in to assist us and becoming the "hollow bone" for them, allows the healing power of the Powers to come through. We are simply channels of their healing power. Long distance ceremonies using the Medicine Wheel are a positive channeling technique. But we can also use our hands for healing when we are in proximity to a plant or animal in need of healing, and even at a distance.

From the Energy Notebook: Ginger's Reiki Healing

Reiki, the Eastern art of hands-on healing, works wonderfully for healing plants and animals. Once you obtain a Reiki attunement, animals will flock to receive the healing energy, and plants will actually bend in your direction! Your aura, implanted with the healing symbols, is changed by the attunement so that plants and animals within the radius of your energy body will instantly recognize your ability as a conduit for healing energy. All animals are energy hogs — especially cats (the first energy workers, which the ancient Egyptians recognized) — instantly able to see and manipulate energy in a person's physical body (that's what the "kneading" is all about).

An example of healing animals with Reiki is my late dog Ginger, a Boykin spaniel. Ginger and I had just moved to my house in Lena. I was undergoing a divorce. Life was not very happy. I was trying to make a new life for myself, and had only just learned Reiki.

One day after coming home from work, I let Ginger out and as I prepared dinner, I heard a horrible noise. I looked out and Ginger had been struck by a car. Her body was mangled and I feared for her life. We rushed to the emergency animal clinic where the veterinarian said he would do what he could and to leave her overnight.

The next day, I went to the vet's office and he said that he had done surgery to put her left rear leg back together, but that her hips were broken, she would probably never walk again and there were internal injuries. She might not live more than a few days. He advised "putting her down." She was, after all, he noted, nine years old.

It was difficult to drive home seeing through the tears, but I could not let Ginger go. She was all I had of the love and joy from my marriage, my only companion and more than a friend. She was the only being I could touch and feel and love. Lying next to me on the car seat, Ginger looked adoringly at me with her big, brown, soulful eyes, so filled with pain and hope. I felt that heroic measures were appropriate. Having only just started practicing Reiki, I said to myself, Well, this is the first real test.

Over the next few days, I practiced Reiki like a madman, applying distance healing when I was at work, hands-on when at home. I appealed to the Powers and practiced every trick in the book for Earth healing, using the house itself as a conduit (Crazy 8s) for a healing environment. At first, there was no response. Ginger couldn't walk, couldn't even move, and, more frightening, as the vet had feared, she had internal injuries and couldn't evacuate waste. I knew this would kill her quickly, with sepsis. I had to massage her abdomen and rectum to release waste from her body. It was a tense few days, requiring every bit of knowledge and skill.

Then, after the fourth day, I came in the front door and a miracle happened. Ginger rose from her bed like a bag of bones and hobbled over to me, slightly dragging her back legs. Her tail was wagging... more a wobble than a wag. But as I knelt to her, she licked my hand and face. Needless to say, I bawled. I knew then she would be all right. And she was. I continued to do Reiki and within days, she was able to make waste on her own and hobble around the house. In three months, she was following her pre-accident routine and able to participate in her favorite hobby: chasing cats! The vet was wrong. She did walk — even run — with no apparent difficulty, except when the weather changed and she would experience some stiffness. She lived for another four years, dying of heart failure — happy, healthy and normal until the end.

I share this story because there are many ways to effectuate healing in energy work. We can all add to our tool boxes or medicine bags. Choose the ways that work for you... alone or in combination.

It's noteworthy in hindsight, the great soul gift Ginger gave to me. Being an adult dog, well past her prime, she knew not to run out into the street. In dog years, after all, she was 56 years old when it happened, and had lived in the city all that time, going everywhere, doing everything. By running out into the street in an All Time/No Time perspective, she taught me how to heal effectively. By sacrificing herself, the nearest, dearest being in my life at a very trying time, she forced me to learn every technique intimately, with an urgency and total dedication that required all my skills and resources and could not be learned any other way. Her sacrifice also jumpstarted my life, pulling me away from my own misery to help and heal others. After Ginger healed, others — people included — started coming for Reiki work, and I was too busy to dwell on my life situation, which quickly and dramatically changed as I changed my focus.

This is how our plant and animal relations help us, by sacrificing themselves and showing us a better way, often only in potential, for everyone.

If only we will listen.

Healing With the Hands

People have been healing with the hands for thousands of years. Even today, many Native peoples do not point or gesture with the hands, instead indicating a person or object by motioning with the mouth, as it was long understood that the hands can be used to give or take energy, the unique medicine of a person, place or thing. Today, the most common form of healing with the hands is Reiki, which was brought to the United States in 1937 by Mrs. Hawayo Takata, a resident of Hawaii. It originated with Mikao Usui in 19th century Japan. Reiki (pronounced ray-key) is a technique for healing and meditation that allows everyone to tap into an unlimited supply of life force energy to improve health and enhance the quality of life. The word "Rei" means "spiritual wisdom." The word "Ki" means "life force energy." Reiki, then, can be called spiritually guided life force energy.

It is "hands on" healing, whereby a Reiki practitioner allows the life force to pass through his or her hands directly to the person, plant or animal in need of healing. It has its own wisdom and goes directly to the area that needs healing. The person who transmits the Reiki energy does not control the healing effect.

Reiki has achieved a status as one of the most popular complementary and alternative medicine modalities. It is used in emergency rooms and by nurses, massage therapists and physical therapists for its proven track record in aiding healing.

Reiki originally came from Japan, but its roots are in Buddhism. It is believed to be an aryuvedic system, although ancient hieroglyphs show it to have been used in Egypt thousands of years ago. It is said that Tibetan monks knew of Reiki in its original form but didn't use its healing effects, instead seeing it as another tool for enlightenment; for they believed that practicing Reiki would alter karma.

Reiki is taught through a master system, where one goes through the major steps of learning and becomes a Reiki master. There commonly are three levels of Reiki:

- Reiki I, whereby the practitioner can heal self and others.

- Reiki II, adds long-distance healing and other techniques.

- Reiki III, the Master level, whereby attunements may be passed on to others.

Different Reiki teachers modify the teachings somewhat, but they all derive from the Reiki technique discovered by Mr. Mikao Usui in 19th century Japan. It is said that the symbols used in healing came to him during a 21-day meditation, or in Native way, a fast, on Mt. Kurama where he received his early Buddhist training. It should come as no surprise that Sensei (teacher) Usui received the knowledge of the Reiki symbols while doing fast at Mount Kurama. By opening himself up to the spirit of the mountain, his 8 became one with the 8 of the mountain, and the mountain spoke to him.

The attunements turn on the healing "switches" encoded in everyone's DNA, so it is a birthright to have this form of healing for everyone. It's simple to learn and intuitive. The Reiki guides do the work, with the Reiki practitioner becoming a "hollow bone" to allow the healing Reiki energy to come through, by focusing intent on the Reiki symbols. As a Reiki master, I highly recommend it. Reiki is easily used in healing plants and animals both in proximity and at a distance, but it does take some training under the guidance of a well-versed practitioner to fully appreciate and perform well. Reiki teachers are plentiful worldwide and training is neither expensive nor demanding, especially in the earlier stages and attunements. It's not necessary to be a Reiki master to use Reiki; master status simply allows one to give attunements and teach others. It does not reflect proficiency so much as increased knowledge.[30]

You do not have to learn Reiki or receive Reiki attunements to heal plants and animals with the hands, either in contact or at a distance. Long before Reiki was commonplace, people were healing plants and animals with the hands both by allowing guides and angels to do the work and/or using the Earthly Mother's own life-force energy. You can do hands-on healing anywhere, in the most urban environment or surrounded by nature. In the urban environment, in a home, apartment or building, you can create a sacred circle and heal with the hands, accessing the Earth energy itself and becoming a conduit for healing power. But it's easier to use the Powers in a natural setting, allowing the natural features of the Earthly Mother and her attendants — the spirits of the land — to do the work.

In accessing the power of the spirits of the land — dakinis (Sanskrit: sky dancer), devas or sprites — it's worth noting that every land form has them, even as land forms themselves have their own spirit. The Sherpa guides of Mt. Everest speak of the spirit of the mountain as being harsh and demanding, something they have learned from interaction with it over hundreds of years. It makes sense, as the 8 of the mountain goes from the lowest to the highest on Earth. Its demands must be great to retain its energetic harmony and balance. But every land form has its own spirit or energy, deriving from sacred geometry; its relationship with all elements within and around it; and a multitude of helping, healing spirits that keep all the land and its beings in balance. From diminutive elementals playing among the flowers, to etheric devas that attend to the plants and trees, to little people who co-exist and interact with the animals... each derives benefit as each gives benefit. All are essential to the Sacred Hoop of Life of the place, and all benefit by what each has to give.

When we do healing ceremony in natural places, we honor these beings and enlist their friendship and support, showing that we are giving what we have to give, and it may be that a spirit of the land may itself have drawn your attention to a plant or animal in need of healing. As Children of Earth and Sky, we each are an intelligent, organizing force. That is our divinity, our medicine, our birthright and our place in the scheme of the Sacred Hoop of Life.

When a plant, animal or spirit being is drawing our attention, it wants our intention — the gift of energy we have to give as a pattern of energy. This can be as simple as mere acknowledgement or something more, such as holding dialogue or doing a healing ceremony. The gift of energy is what is required, for our 8 is the power that is requested: bringing balance with our pattern of energy to the energy that surrounds us. A simple acknowledgement may be enough, just acknowledge and let go of the connection. Acknowledge and let go. But we may also do more profound energy work by enlisting the Powers and the spirits of the land, allowing their energy into our 8 to make it more powerful, inclusive and effective for bringing healing, wholeness, balance and harmony to the Earth and her beings.

The next step is taking our spirit form and using it to heal the spirit form of plants and animals with the art of seeing.

From the Energy Notebook:
Allow, Accept, Acknowledge and Be Grateful

Plants and animals can unite with the Powers of Earth and Sky to communicate many things, on many levels, if you allow them.

On October 28, 2004, I received a message from the trees, the rocks, the plants, the animals, the Powers of Earth and Sky that stays with me still. It was the night of the Full Lunar Eclipse, and Spirit kept tugging at me to do special ceremony: not ceremony for the people, per se, but for healing the self. So, I went out to the Bear Lodge, our Asi (Cherokee, "hot house")/Inipi (Lakota, "purification" lodge), planning to do personal sweat. Spirit told me to bring my Bear skin, the one I wear while dancing the Bear, and my pipe (chanupa).

Once I arrived, though, Spirit (intuition/inner guidance) told me that I was not there to "sweat," but to be one with the Earth while the eclipse was under way. I walked about 100 yards from the Lodge and sat on a slight rise where I could see each direction for some distance, and wrapped myself in my bear skin. As the shadow of the Earth began nibbling at the Moon, I began drumming, slow and deep, keeping a cadence that echoed the hidden power of the Earth. After that, I know not, for I was transported into a different world.

Wrapped in my bear skin, my pipe to my heart, the drum in my hands, I went deeper and deeper and deeper... until all was totally dark and still... total peace, total serenity... a silence so full... then, a blinding white flash!

Next thing I knew, it was two hours later. I was not asleep. It was as if only an instant had passed — the blink of an eye — yet, paraded before me in that flash of an instant that spanned two hours was every person I had ever known... and would know... my God self... all, one, in diversity, all pieces to the whole.

I stood and listened to a roaring silence of all beings around me, one with every plant, tree, bird, animal. It was if all their voices were one; the very sky spoke wordlessly of healing and wholeness. And before me, I looked, and it appeared as if the line of trees in the distance were advancing toward me, the ground melting away. I could hear every leaf speaking, the voices of them all, as one chorus. And the trees told me: Allow, Accept, Acknowledge and Be Grateful.

These things, all things around us compete for our attention. There is great suffering in the world and sorrow. Personal fortunes rise and fall, hopes are built, and dashed, triumphs are hard won and forgotten in an instant, but there is only one reality: the heart. The heart which speaks: Allow, Accept, Acknowledge and Be Grateful to hold, give, take, exist and be whole, as a living embodiment of love, health, healing and wholeness.

After a while, the trees melted back into the distance, and hearing returned in this world; the Sky Paths of the Holy Ones began to recede. The Moon, once so all-encompassing, in both light and darkness, receded to a hard, cold, bright ball far in the inky blackness of the sky, with indifferent stars around it, and I felt a chill. It was again just a cold, dark night, filled with the dampness of dew and a slight shivering breeze. Not wanting to let go of the moment, I drummed some, danced some, gave thanks and prayers for every being.

I spoke aloud my thoughts and thanks and gratitude and was certain every being on Earth heard it, took it to heart.

Allow, Accept, Acknowledge and Be Grateful. Yes. That is the way.

Thank you, Creator, all beings. Aho.

Review

How to heal plants near and far:

- Recognize that the world is a sacred circle, or medicine wheel, and you are at the center of it, affecting every being, and all is one in the Medicine Wheel of the World; there is no "near" and "far" when you are one.

- Recognize that you have a place within the sacred circle of the world, and the world reflects what you think of it, how you feel, and what you do as part of the universal hologram; this medicine that you carry is The Healing Medicine Wheel.

- Exercise your "butterfly wings" to create Crazy 8s, the *heyoka* energy of healing, by "listening" within, and dialoguing with plants and animals.

- Welcome the Powers and learn from them.

Internet key words: *hologram, tesseract, fractals, medicine wheel, heyoka, kachina.*

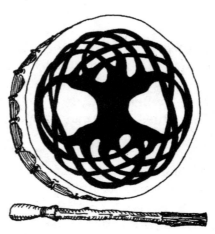

Chapter Three

The Shamanic Journey

The tree which moves some to tears of joy is
inthe eyes of others only a green thing
which stands in the way. ... As the eye is
formed, such are its powers.
— WILLIAM BLAKE, 1799

Learning to listen, as we discussed in Chapter Two, is only one way of understanding, healing and helping plants and animals. Learning to see is important, as well, and no practice is as useful for seeing as the shamanic journey. People often say, "I would like to learn how to do that, but it seems so hard." That is ego/personality talking. If you can daydream or night dream, you can journey shamanically. It's only a matter of learning a few techniques and practicing.

Several people and organizations teach how to journey shamanically and numerous books are available.[1] The easiest way to journey is to remember your Crazy 8s. Consider the above circle and the below circle, with you in the middle. Where the above circle and below circle meet is where you are; it is you, and your world around you. These circles correspond with the upper world, the lower world and the middle world. The easiest way to enter the shamanic state is through drumming. You can drum or listen to someone else, or use a recording with shamanic drumming on it. Shamanic drumming has its own beat, about 70 beats per minute.[2] In Native way, the drumming is called the heartbeat of the Earth Mother, and this is true. Whether fast or slow, the drum creates harmonics of the pulse of the Earth in its energy. When we consciously drum to accentuate the energy of the Earth, a doorway opens into non-ordinary reality, allowing the energies to connect within us, for ceremony or ceremonial dancing in the physical world, or "riding the drum" outward into the world or worlds of shamanic journey. Learning to drum and journey at the same time takes considerable practice; it's easier to have someone else drum or listen to a recording. You can record yourself drumming for use in journeying, but a bit of practice is required to keep a steady tempo for a prolonged period without losing track, being distracted, or journeying off yourself while you do it. You must maintain the right attitude throughout the drumming so that the energy is kept constant and supportive of journeying.

The mechanics of journeying are quite simple; the harmonics allow us to "ride the drum" as it were, while they also raise our vibration rate and lull the conscious mind. This is why drumming is also useful to connect with spirits, consecrate or clear lands and promote healing.[3] The poor Coyote mind gets bored, goes to sleep or wanders off, allowing who we really are — the authentic self, the one who listens — to come forward, lured by the beat of the Earthly Mother. The matter at hand, then, is intent. Remember that the shaman's primary duty — indeed, the very essence of shamanism — is to practice discernment and carefully direct intent.

In shamanism, intent is everything. If you intend to journey, you will journey.

Shamanic journeying requires no drugs or "medicine" of any kind, except your own medicine. All the chemicals you require are already in your brain. Although the results, the visions, insights, abilities, can be fantastic, utterly and truly "out of this world," the ability to journey shamanically is every human being's birthright. Again, if you can dream, or daydream, you can journey. There is nothing esoteric about it, despite what some would make it out to be; it is simply viewing the world in a different way or, more accurately, allowing ourselves to view the world in a different way. I've taught, or helped teach, hundreds of people how to journey and all have been able to journey, although some have needed more help than others.[4]

It might help to become proficient at journeying by simultaneously consciously exploring nighttime dreaming, that is, going to Dreamtime, and "seeing" there. Keep a notepad by your bed, and just before going to sleep resolve to remember all dreams and write them down immediately upon waking. Over time, not only will you automatically begin recalling dreams but you will consciously participate in them, thus gaining more insight into their meaning and increasing power over your consciousness. To do this, apply the simple yet effective technique taught to Carlos Castaneda by his teacher, Don Juan: while dreaming, remember to look for your hands, because when you find them you can control the dream.[5]

Again, in most ways of teaching shamanism, the universe is defined as three worlds: the upper, middle and lower worlds. There are, of course, infinite worlds, but this is a good framework for understanding. The upper world can be seen as the place where angels reside, where Jack climbed the Beanstalk in nursery tales, the place that's "up there," heaven, with clouds, etc., where higher beings are found. In my own journeys into the upper world, I see myself shooting up from the Earth, seeing the globe fall away, as the continents become tiny, and passing through a layer of energy to actually reach the upper world, which is more or less in space, but seen a bit differently than portrayed by astronauts and satellite photos. This layer of energy is the marker point between the Earth and the upper world in non-ordinary reality; some call it the Christ Consciousness Grid or the Plume of Quetzalcoatl, or the Akashic Field.[6] Once having passed through this permeable layer, you are definitely in non-ordinary reality and can go anywhere.[7]

The lower world is characterized as a dark place deep within the Earth. It has been described in myth and folklore as the place where other realities can be found, such as the River Styx, where the dead "cross over," as the place where Pluto reigns and Persephone travels to while the energies of the surface are in winter and life is below, and where magical, mystical beings reside. It's going down the rabbit hole in *Through the Looking-Glass,* where everything is topsy-turvy, with its own illogical laws and improbable, though powerful denizens.[8] Indeed, in shamanic journey, this is where power animals reside and a shaman is sometimes asked to go there to retrieve a power animal. Often, what is not told, though, is that it is through the underworld where one can travel through time; visiting the Earth or other worlds at any time in past or future. It's not the "dark" place some would imagine, but actually capable of hosting any number of realities. It is in this place, for example, where we store the soul pieces that have been stolen from others through many lifetimes. One of the exercises a shaman learns in soul retrieval is how to release the pieces gathered over centuries, so that they may return to where they belong, thus freeing the shaman of the oppressive energetic influences of karmic debt. Returning lost soul pieces is a unique branch of shamanism whereby practitioners retrieve energetic pieces that have been lost, usually through trauma. Energy is shed so that the person does not feel all the pain; but the body knows that pieces are missing. In most Native American cultures, warriors, for example, would not be allowed to mingle with the general population until they had been cleansed of all negative energy and soul pieces that had been lost were returned. Sometimes, soul pieces are stolen. In ancient days, shamans would steal souls to frighten their enemies or weaken them. Nowadays, most "stolen" soul pieces are usually inadvertent; a person pining for a lost love, for example, might give away soul essence to the object of devotion, a harried young mother who is tired might look at her bouncing baby and wish she had some of that vitality. These are usually minor losses and gains. No one benefits from taking soul pieces; they belong to the person and cannot be used in any meaningful way by someone else. But sometimes a shaman must steal back soul pieces from someone who has taken them.

Here on Earth, we live in what is seen through the lens of the shamanic experience as the middle world. This is where we want to journey to see the plants and animals that share our world, listen to what they have to tell us and perhaps learn their songs and their secrets, so that we can help and heal them and others.

Exercise 8 Accessing Non-Ordinary Reality

The steps for shamanic journey are very simple. Most people begin to learn how to journey by traveling to the underworld to meet their power animal.[9] The power animal is a being — actually, a power of the universe — that accompanies you wherever you go. We are each born with one to attend to us. Remember that fuzzy bear you carried around as a child? Or the unicorn? Or the tiger? That was probably your power animal — or totem — from birth. We usually refer to power animals as animals, because animals are universal upon this planet and have recognizable qualities — such as bears and tigers being fierce protectors, while also furry and cuddly — but the attending power can be anything. Although your totem may last throughout your lifetime, power animals come and go. Usually, you have at least one, though some people — shamans particularly — can have whole menageries.

So, to begin, turn on your tape or CD of drumming, or have a friend drum a steady beat for you, approximately 70 beats per minute. (Any type of drum is fine, although a single-sided, hand drum is easy to hold for long periods. Remo makes a wonderful synthetic drum called the Buffalo Drum, which in 16-inch diameter works well in all weathers, is inexpensive compared with hand-crafted leather drums, and travels well on airplanes. For more information, see the author's Web site: www.blueskywaters.com.

Start with a journey of 15 minutes. It may be useful to cover your eyes with a cloth to block out the light. Lie down, take a few deep breaths and clear your mind. Imagine yourself in a cool, dark place, a waiting place, a good place to begin your journey. It could be a cave or a place on a beach that you particularly enjoy. The main thing is that you want to have a hole nearby that you can go down into. Perhaps there is a tree with a hole in it in a park near your house. Or it could be a bridge near your home that is dark underneath. Some people even go down the kitchen drain!

After you have gained some proficiency at journeying, it is here where your power animal will come to greet you, at this waiting place, to take you above or below or outward into one of the three worlds. But this time we want to go down the hole, whatever it may be, to meet your power animal. It could very well be that your power animal will show up now, even before you have entered the hole. It could be any type of animal, but you will recognize it for its friendliness; it will exude an aura of goodness — no sharp teeth or threatening mannerisms. It will also show you at least three different aspects of itself; for example, sideways, frontward and backwards. In Native way, when an animal shows itself to you in one of its sacred poses, like the Coyote in three-quarter profile on a hill, it is lending you its power, and showing you that you are connected. Your power animal will seek to show you that it belongs to you and you belong to it, in this way.

If your power animal shows itself to you in this waiting place, that's fine. Go with it, but if not, then imagine going down the hole you have chosen, going down, down, down, past roots of trees, through rocks. Remember, you are in spirit form, you can go through anything, or around anything, or jump over anything — there is no limit to your powers, getting big or getting small, as the need arises. Keep going down, down, down, until you finally arrive somewhere. You will know you are there because you will stop. Look around. It's likely you will see many power animals and beings; or you may see none at all. Whatever you see, look at it for future reference. But if there are many beings, remember that your power animal will show itself to you in three different poses, and its energy will be one of connection and support.

Once your power animal connects with you, allow it to take you for a journey; hop on its back, or let it guide you as you fly. The sky isn't the limit; the horizons are endless. After 15 minutes, have your friend drum you back, that is, double the tempo of the drum with the intent of energetically pulling you back into this reality. Your friend should say, "OK, time to come back!" And you should wiggle your toes and stretch your fingers, allowing all your energy to come back into your body.

When you have come back, relate what you have seen; write it down for future reference. Often, while in shamanic journey, what you see may not make a great deal of sense. But in shamanic journey, everything is symbolic. Having a vision of a wall, for example, may not be a physical wall, but a barrier that you are experiencing in your life. If there was writing on the wall that said something like "look for blue skies," it could mean that the solution to that problem in your life will be solved by a place, activity or behavior relating to blue skies. Suppose you were having difficulty at work and had been thinking about taking a trip to the beach, but it seemed there was so much to do at work that you couldn't get away. The message would be: go to the beach, the barriers preventing you from moving forward will dissolve then.

It should be noted that the area of the brain used for seeing in shamanic journey is adjacent to the area of imagination. So, the best way to learn how to see in shamanic journey, if you have difficulty, is to use your imagination at first. That is, imagine that you are going down into the underworld; imagine that you are seeing a power animal, etc. As time goes by, and you repeatedly journey, you will find that there is less "imagination" and more dreaming or journeying, which is "real." It's a question of quality; simply slipping over from suggesting (imagining) visions or insights, to actually having visions and insights seemingly unbidden.

Exercise 9 Learning to See

"You make this sound so easy," some people complain to me about learning this work. Well, it is easy. All of it. It's all about learning to "see." In this, and everything. It's all the heyoka way. Seeing literally what is before your face. Try this: hold your splayed hand palm toward you about one inch from your face. What do you see?

It looks like a big blur, and you can't see anything beyond it.

Now, focus between your fingers and move your head a little from side to side. What do you see?

You can see everything; you just have to shift a little.

Now, remove your hand. What do you see?

You see everything you saw before but without anything blocking your view.

In our lives we tend to focus on what is in front of us. We often find blockages, huge, insurmountable obstacles that seem to have no solution. All it takes is shifting your focus. Don't look at what is blocking you; look for what is beyond, what comes into focus without the obstacle in front of you. Don't focus on the "buts" or "if onlys" or any of the whys of "I can't" or "it won't." Focus on what you plan to achieve, desire or find needful.

If you focus on what is beyond the immediate, not on the blockage, not on what you know, or think you know, but on what you seek, you will see what you need to see and the blockage will fade away or you will remove it. Try it. In life. In everything. That's learning to "see."

From the Energy Notebook: On the Back of an Eagle

Learning to journey changed my world. As I've mentioned, all of my life I had "seen" things in nightly dreaming and intuited events in the waking state. It was a born gift and a curse, in that I could not control it. As a result, I tried to block it and sublimate it, stuff it down. But learning to journey, which a friend introduced me to by reading about it in a book, changed everything. I will never forget it. My friend said that she had attended a workshop where they had performed shamanic journey, using a drum. I scoffed, "How could that be?" She persisted and said, "Let's try it." So, she had me read the steps of how to journey from the book.[10] Then, she began to beat the drum in a steady cadence, and before I could say "Jack Spratt" I was off into non-ordinary reality. As the drum started, with my eyes closed, I saw nothing, only darkness, with thoughts such as "Why am I doing this", "This is fruitless, I don't know what I'm doing", "This won't work". But as the drum continued its cadence, the thoughts began to subside. I was lulled into a sense of comfort by the beats and then, before I knew it, an eagle appeared before me. It said, wordlessly, "Climb on my back." I did so and we took off into the air, flying over a landscape of rolling hills covered with trees. I know now that I was in the underworld, and this was one of four power animals that routinely accompany me on journeys — the eagle for major events, the bear who is always there but doesn't always show, the wolf that is always there but rarely shows, and the owl, which comes when called. In this journey, we surveyed the land and I thrilled with the experience of flying. It was like so many dreams I had had, but seemed more real because it was immediate, it was "now." We flew for a while, and then circled a low valley. The eagle landed and I hopped off. I didn't know what I was doing there, but felt good. The trees and grasses were vibrant green, full of life that I could touch and feel without touching. They were welcoming and we had a dialogue that was at the same time subliminal, constant and available for more if wanted. I wandered through this forest until I came to a wooded ravine with a babbling brook running through it. Across the brook, on a small island bordered by the waterway bending around it, I saw an old man with a beard in three-quarter profile. The man appeared so calm, knowledgeable and wise. He was holding a staff and sitting before a small fire that seemed to speak to him. He seemed able to communicate to the fire, the two doing a dance of understanding between them. I turned to the eagle and asked, "Who is that man?" The eagle replied,

"That is you, in 10 years."

I was astounded. How could I be such a man as that? My life was in turmoil. I was constantly besieged by problems, worries, health issues, every woe imaginable. Yet, here was this calm, knowledgeable, wise man — someone whom I could admire and trust. "Surely, that's not me," I protested. The eagle laughed, "It is you."

With that, I climbed upon the back of the eagle again and we flew off, returning to wherever it was that we had come from, and I came out of the journey with the sound of the drum calling me back, and my friend asking, "Well, did you see anything?"

I'm not sure what I said then, but I can say now, what I saw came true.

Your Power Animal: Don't Leave Home Without It

Once you have met your power animal, always remember not to leave home without it! It is a Power of the Universe and will protect you from all harm, no matter how great the potential threat. If nothing else, it will sling you into another universe to escape harm, allowing you to return safely. This goes for Dreamtime, too. In nighttime journey, connect with your power animal; simply ask it to appear, and it will. Whether you call this way of seeing astral travel, shamanic journey or simply dreaming, it is important that we call upon the Powers to guide and protect us, so that we may see and learn safely. It's a big universe — or universes! — out there. Not all we may meet are gentle, kind or have our best interests in mind.

Some people have asked, "Aren't you afraid that teaching someone to journey without going with them will cause a problem?" No, because we all have a power animal, at least one, who is watching over us all the time. You can bet that in All Time/No Time, which is the real world, your power animal knows when you are going to journey for the first time before you do. It will be there, but you must ask to see it. In all this work, with the Powers, with guides, angels, power animals, you first must ask; that is a universal law. As Children of Earth and Sky, we are powerful beings; we were sent here for a purpose, and even if we don't recognize our purpose, and walk like cattle upon the Earth with our heads down to the ground, unconscious and unknowing, we still have higher powers that watch over us. It's up to us to recognize them and appeal to them to show themselves and help us.

It's very rare that a person does not have a power animal; occasionally, someone will come to me to retrieve one for them. But the symptoms of not having a power animal are very clear: if every imaginable thing that can go wrong goes wrong, repeatedly, it's likely you have lost your power animal or are between power animals. In that case, it may be useful to find a shaman and have him or her retrieve one for you by going into the lower world and finding one that is willing. It could be one from an earlier time, perhaps from youth, or one that is more pertinent to your current stage in life. But you can call a power animal to you, as well. Create your sacred circle, unfold your butterfly wings and think of any animal that meant something to you from your childhood: it may be the cuddly teddy bear, or monkey or dragon — anything that you slept with, chewed on, dragged around with you or wouldn't let your parents take away, even in the bathtub. That likely is your totem, and it should always be with you or within call. Simply call, with your heart, and it will come. You may feel goose bumps when it arrives — which we jokingly call truth bumps, since it's automatic in our nervous systems that when something touches us energetically, we get goose bumps. Then, you will feel a sigh of relief. Know that it is there. If you journey, you will find it, too. Once you have connected with your power animal, or totem, in this way, pay homage to it: put pictures of the animal or being, or one like it — perhaps cut from a magazine or printed out from the Internet — on your refrigerator, desk, altar or carry one around in your purse or pocket. Power animals are like stray cats, if you feed them, in this case, with heart-felt gratitude and appreciation, they tend to hang around. Also, read about the characteristics of the animal. Notice which qualities it possesses that you share, and which ones are qualities you desire, and ask the power animal to help you in these matters. You will be surprised what comes your way.

From the Energetic Notebook: The Owl and The Stone People

A number of years ago, a friend and I were on a trip to Oklahoma, and part of our trip was to look for interesting rocks — grandfathers, stone people — that we could bring back with us. As we were driving through the Glass Mountains, we noticed the gravel by the highway had a sheen like glass. We pulled over and began picking through the stones, asking if any wanted to come along. At this time, the owl had come to me as a power animal; it is the shaman's totem. Although some Native people fear the owl, thinking it brings death, which is a corruption of what it represents. The owl walks between the worlds and is able to see beyond the veil. Shamans appeal to the owl, and the owl to the shaman, because the word shaman itself is Siberian for "one who sees in the dark." Death may appear to be darkness to those who do not see beyond the veil, but to the shaman, death is just another reality. Part of a shaman's training is to experience his or her own death and come back again; then, there is no fear of death, only knowledge. This knowledge the shaman shares with the owl. And, indeed, in Cherokee, the owl is considered one of the most sacred of beings, among those who know the true history of the people, for it was one of the few animals that stayed awake during the seven days of Creation. So, we were picking through these stones by the side of the road when out of nowhere, it seemed, a woman drove up on an all-terrain vehicle. "Whatcha doing?" she asked. "We're looking for interesting rocks," we replied, not knowing to what extent to reveal our interest. We made idle chat for a while and then she said, "Well, if you really want interesting rocks, we've got a bunch on our place. Follow me!"

So, we followed her in our vehicle down a winding, dirt road, at times perilously steep with great drop offs on one side or another, until we came to a field that was filled with the most magical stones you could imagine: giant sheets of crystal clear isinglass literally growing from the earth, some several feet tall. "Take all you want," she said. "Then, when you're through, come on back to the house," she added, pointing down another dirt trail, "and I'll fix you something to eat."

We gathered pieces of isinglass in sacred manner, asking which ones wanted to go with us, one from here, one from there, until we had a small pile, and then exhausted, we drove to the woman's house. Approaching the front door, I wondered, "How on Earth did we find this woman? What an incredible experience!" But, as she let us in the entryway, it became clear. I had to laugh. She must have thought me utterly crazy, but there in the hallway by the front door was a bookshelf with row upon row of ceramic owls. Hundreds of them.

Thank you, I whispered to *our* power animal.

Those sheets of isinglass that we gathered, now grace the front steps to our house.

Exercise 10 The Middle World Journey

Now that you have successfully met your power animal, it is time for a middle world journey. You may wish to go out longer than 15 minutes, perhaps 30 or even 45 minutes. Repeat the steps of starting the drumming and going to your place where you meet your power animal. Sometimes, I find that my power animal is a little tardy in showing up. That's fine. We're in no hurry here. If you were to record your journey, describing what you see out loud, you would find that most of the 15 to 30 minutes that is the average journey is spent in silence. The actual shamanic journey is spent in All Time/No Time, so the images or information are often jammed into a few seconds, faster than you can speak or describe. (If using a tape recorder, it's best to have one that has the voice activation feature to avoid long pauses.) It's akin to REM sleep, where a person actually only dreams every 45 minutes or so, when the eyelids are fluttering; the rest of the time is spent in unconsciousness. If your power animal is tardy in showing up, it might be useful to find a tone to silently hum as a calling signature. For example, when my Bear is tardy, I start humming a wordless tune that sounds something like a mosquito. We both know that it's a joking way to say "I am here and I'm ready to journey!" You may find that tones themselves have power in non-ordinary reality — able to blast down walls or summon storms. Your very voice can command events of unimaginable diversity. The tone of OM, for example, can create whole worlds in some instances.

When your power animal shows up, ask it to take you around your house, perhaps room to room or maybe overhead and around and then to points of interest in the house. Some objects will appear very large or assume a different shape altogether; their power is different in non-ordinary reality — or All Time/No Time — than in physical reality. Some of the objects may have messages for you: symbols or intuitions about where they come from, how they might be better used, if they should be given to someone else or other issues about their power or medicine.

You may see living beings that are not present in ordinary reality but that inhabit your home, such as spirits or perhaps fragments (ghosts).[11] You will find that your abode is a living organism, as well as a space that can hold within it many other spaces, or dimensions. You may even find vortexes that allow portals into other dimensions within your home that you may have intuited, for example, a closet that seems to have things appear or disappear, or a room that always gives you a funny feeling.

It's worth noting that you may not be able to see at all when you are in shamanic journey. It's not unusual for someone who is very visually oriented, say a photographer or artist, to not be able to see in the visual sense, since that ability is already highly developed in a set energetic pattern; instead you may see with your nose. Consider that a dog or wolf can identify some odors at as little as one part per trillion (1 part per 1,000,000,000,000), not only "seeing" molecules through the sense of smell, but differentiating between them. The area of the canine brain that deals with the olfactory sense is much larger than that of humans and exceedingly well developed, as well as the nostrils and hairs and nerve endings within the nostrils, so that canines (and bears, too) actually see through smell: call it smellovision. It's useful to remember when dealing with animals that visions may be more akin to smelling than seeing. But humans don't appreciate their sense of smell, often sublimating that sense, which may come forward during a shamanic journey. Actually, the sense of smell has close connections with areas of the brain associated with memory. So, if you see through smelling, don't worry. It may actually give you a better sense of the world in ordinary reality by allowing your brain to process information in a more holistic manner, linking phenomena more directly to your past experiences or qualitative and emotional judgment for a more accurate reading of your experiences in non-ordinary reality. Also, one journey may be through smell, as altered as it may be through expanded sense awareness; the next through intuition, or a sense of knowing; and the next through actual physical sensation. Just relax and allow your power animal to show you your world. It will be transmitted in the easiest way possible for you to process, if you allow it without worry.

Chapter Four

Applications

The survival of the world depends on
our sharing what we have, and working together.
If we do not, the whole world will die.
First the planet, and next the people.

—Frank Fools Crow, Lakota Medicine Man

This final chapter is all about learning to "be." That is, practicing that which you know. Do the exercises and perform the applications. If you don't feel you have succeeded, try again later. As they say, Rome wasn't built in a day, so keep doing them; no effort is wasted. There is no pressure here, no deadlines, no "get it right, right now." Learning is a process, sometimes a slow one, but one day you will discover that all that you once might have thought you couldn't do suddenly has become effortless, done without thinking. Forgive yourself and laugh if you fail, for you have not failed; you simply haven't reached where you think you ought to be. Looking back, you may find that it was the *trying* that was difficult, the action and accomplishment was easy. And it will be the accomplishment, not the trying, not the failing, that will grow and endure, gaining strength and power. Don't let negative self talk convince you that your efforts aren't working or are in any way in vain.

Remember, all energy work is in All Time/No Time, so effects may not come when expected; they may occur in the future, or may have already happened without you knowing. There is also the law of unintended consequences. If you focus on one thing to happen, it may be that the result is another thing which is ultimately more beneficial. Also, all efforts are cumulative. Energy is neither created nor destroyed, but is transmuted. It may make the long, lazy 8 in another way than anticipated. But don't give up. Thomas Edison once said, "Many of life's failures are people who did not realize how close they were to success when they gave up."

Realize that you already are successful merely by doing. The result may come unexpectedly, and quickly, in a time and way you never could have expected. In this, we do the best we can, but we always "give it to Creator" with gratitude. Gratitude is the strongest aspect of our personal force, allowing miracles and allowing us to be co-creators with Creator. Results we cannot control. That is beyond our control; it is Creator, and the Powers, the Flow of Creation that do this work, not us. We want to put ourselves in the position of allowing Creator to create in a good way, using our attention and intention to facilitate balance, harmony, health and wholeness in ways where we can participate, helping define the flow for good results.

This walk with the nations, learning to hear, learning to see, learning to be, is not over. It is just begun.

Balancing Your Body: Being the Eagle

Before connecting with Earth Energy for healing in proximity or a distance, it may be helpful to balance the energies of your body. In the normal course of the day, our energetic systems may go out of balance, but it's easy to balance the energies. First, smudge yourself either with the smoke of white sage or cedar or use a liquid smudge that contains the essence of sacred plants if you are allergic to smoke or are in a place where fire may not be used.

Calm the mind and breathe slowly, in and out, in and out, allowing the Earth energy to flow up through your feet and Creator's energy to flow from above through the top of your head (your crown chakra.) Ground, center and shield.

Then, stretch your arms in front of you slightly below the level of your waist and turn your palms outward so the backs of the hands are opposite each other. Cross your arms and clasp your hands together, interlocking your fingers, and with one movement bring your clasped hands up to your chest with your elbows tight against your body. Hold this position and breathe slowly, releasing whatever tension may be in your body and whatever thoughts may be crowding your mind. When thoughts come to mind, just push them out with your breath, allowing the good energy of the Earthly Mother to come in through your crown and feet. After a few moments, when you feel clear, move your clasped hands down again and unlock your fingers; hold your arms straight out from your body, like the wings of a flying eagle, and shake your fingers, allowing energy to be released. You may also pull the energy from your fingers, like pulling taffy, and toss it to the Earth Mother.

Children often do this backward clasping of the hands intuitively, knowing when the energy of their body is out of balance and naturally bringing it back into alignment. It can be done anytime, of course, not only when preparing to heal plants and animals. Yoga practitioners may wish to do the same thing using The Eagle (*Garuda* in Sanskrit) pose, which brings balance to the body, mind and spirit. To perform it, draw the left foot up, bending the knee, and wrap it around the right leg. Then, cross arms at the elbows, left over right. Join the palms of your hands together keeping the fingers pointed upward. Breathe. Then, return to normal. Repeat the exercise wrapping the right leg over the left leg and right arm over left arm.

Being One with All That Is

A simple way of being one with All That Is would be to simply find a place in nature and lie down, being one with Earth Mother. Again, this is something that little children do, along with digging in the Earth, just to see what's there, that opens our hearts to simply being. If you grew up with pronounced seasons, remember when you were young and raking leaves in the fall, again a simple exercise of being. Remember how wonderful it was, after heaping the leaves, to run and jump into the pile, burrowing deep, smelling the rich odors of the plants and earth, rolling around in them, hearing their crunching sounds and rolling over to see the sky and clouds high above. You are never too old to enjoy the natural sights, sounds, feeling of the Earth and Sky. But it's a wise person who can drink deeply of this cup that the world offers, including the profound wisdom of innocent youth. Try simply lying on the ground and feeling with all your senses, the wonders all around, reaching deep with your energetic body into the Earth, and reaching high to touch the clouds, being one with All That Is.

Creating a Sacred Circle

Creating a sacred circle is a very important aspect of increasing the effectiveness of healing, since it focuses your energies, leads to right thinking and sets intent. Choose a place of power — a location in nature that is secluded or with a vista that feels right — where your energies are most conducive to the sacred geometry of the land forms.[1] Walk straight out from this place to the east, about ten feet, or however large you want your sacred circle to be, then walk clockwise, stopping at each cardinal direction to feel the energies. Walk around this circle four times, each time singing or praying in thanks to the Creator and all beings for having this opportunity to share body, mind, heart and soul, and sprinkling tobacco or cornmeal to form the perimeter of the circle. On the first round, you may wish to shake a rattle to break up the energies that are there, so they may conform to your sacred intent. Then, on the last round, light sage or cedar and walk clockwise in a spiral toward the center, waving the smoke to fill the circle.

Afterwards, do as you are guided, performing the desired ceremony, or if you prefer, meditating or simply enjoying the sanctity of nature.

Enlisting the Powers

When we do sacred ceremony, we enlist the Powers to come help us. Ceremonies can be elaborate, with many features and a great deal of healing for plants or animals or they may be as simple as giving thanks. But in order to enlist the Powers, we must create a sacred space for them. Here is an example (for more, see my first two books, *Clearing*, and *Finding Sanctuary in Nature*).

First, create a sacred circle. Once the circle is complete, sit in the east, facing west, and invite in each of the Directions —the *unoli* — thanking them for joining with you in the healing ceremony. You may wish to put five stones before you to devise a Medicine Wheel: one for the center and one for each of the directions. Thank all of your guides, angels, power animals, the powers of Earth and Sky, the ancestors and divine beings for being present and helping you in this healing ceremony. Acknowledge the directions — the Four Harmonies — for correcting any mistakes you may make, or deficiencies of knowledge, so that the healing takes place. You are a hollow bone in this ceremony; it is not you doing the healing, you are allowing the divine Powers to do their work. You may rattle, drum or sing to invite them in, and thank them for the healing, if you are guided.

A prayer might go like this, but use your own heart to determine the words you use and Powers you invite:

Dear Lord Creator, Earthly Mother, Heavenly Father, Guides, Angels, Power Animals, Ancestors, Goddesses and Divine Beings of Light, thank you for allowing us to be here and to do this work. We are grateful for your presence and healing help, and thank you for all you do.

Creator, thank you for your divine light and for giving us life, and everything.

Earthly Mother, we thank you for all that you provide us for life, the land, the water, the very air we breathe, all things.

Guides, thank you for speaking so that we may hear you, and follow what you have to say, so that this great healing takes place.

Angels, thank you for your beautiful miracles above, below and all around, backwards and forwards in time — even miracles we do not see or know but do take place.

Power animals, we thank you for your connections and protections and for keeping out all negativity, bringing us what we need, and as powers of the universe, lending your power to this healing.

Ancestors we thank you for smiling upon us and the work we do this day, allowing the healing to go before us and behind us, so that all within our Sacred Circle are healed.

Goddesses, and Divine Beings of Light, we are most grateful for your miracles of Earth and Sky, and thank you for shining your light upon us, so that our voices are heard and the world brought in balance in all ways. We thank you for this day, this moment, and this Circle of Light to help all beings.

The prayer may be as long or as short as your heart tells, speaking from the heart. Remember, the heart is circular, not literal; it doesn't matter what you say as much as how you say it and that it operates to open the heart, clear the mind and connect with the Powers, allowing them in and creating a sacred space within for healing to occur. Make sure and thank the ancestors. By saying "ancestors" we are not merely thanking all who came before, but all who will come afterward. We each are only a point in the Sacred Hoop of Life which goes backwards and forwards in time. By thanking the ancestors, we are enlisting powers, abilities and healing that have yet to be as well as that which has already occurred, creating a spiral of All Time/No Time with beneficial effects for all beings in all times and all places, healing all.

Once the prayers and supplications are done, you may do whatever healing ceremony is required, if in contact with the plant or animal within the circle, or at a distance by using an object to represent the plant or animal.

Once the healing ceremony is complete, thank the Powers and deconstruct the circle by walking around it four times counterclockwise, giving thanks in prayer or song, and releasing the energies and the space.

Hands-On Healing With Earth Energy: Stretching Your Butterfly Wings

You can do this hands-on healing outdoors, indoors or anywhere. Put yourself in your sacred circle. Ground, center, shield. Breathe. Take a few deep breaths. Clear your mind. Imagine the energy from your spine, where your bottom meets the Earth, as going down, down, down into the Earthly Mother, connecting with a crystalline cave deep within her. Imagine the sacred circle around you being the Golden Mean Spiral, connecting all that vibrates into this plane of existence and going on beyond into the next, reaching upward, eternally, from plane to plane of existence, like the coils of the twin snakes of the caduceus or the twin helix spiral of DNA, each loop, or Crazy 8, connecting you with the above and below. You are one with this world, and connected with all others. Around you is a contained sphere, your energy, reaching out as far as you wish, connecting with whatever you wish, near or far. You are safe and protected within this sacred circle. See your energy as a beautiful figure 8, with you in the center, the above world the top circle, the below world the bottom circle. You are one with all the energies of Earth and Sky, your energy circling around below, bringing to the surface the beautiful energy of the Earthly Mother, spiraling through you, circling above, connecting with the Christ Consciousness Grid, the Plume of Quetzalcoatl, the highest energies of all that is and can be upon the Earth. And you are at the center of all of this. Imagine, if you wish, that you have butterfly wings. This is the Crazy 8 going out from you, all around you, here, there, everywhere, in every direction, flitting here, there, everywhere, so fast it cannot be seen. Extend your butterfly wings. Be one with everything. Within this circle, you may wish to connect with a plant or animal that is dear to you, within your sight or touch, or it could be far away. Distances mean nothing when you are connected with everything. You are within a circle of Power, and all things, all beings, every plant, rock, tree is a part of you. Where you direct your attention is where you touch, where you heal, where you bring balance, healing, wholeness. Even if it's just a tendril of thought going out, let it follow your intention to where you want it to go, to connect with the plant or animal. Allow the love and joy of that plant or animal to become a part of you and you a part of it. Give blessings, connecting with the beings of the Earth and Sky, allowing their heart/soul to connect, uplift and brighten the plant or animal. Imagine the plant or animal in its spirit form. If its DNA were a sequence of code, it would be producing an image of itself in its perfect state at this time. Focus on the image that is its perfect state. Imagine a photograph of it, if that makes imaging it easier. You are the camera recording the spirit form, and taking the spirit form that you see within you and projecting it, you allow it to become one with the plant or animal, if the plant or animal will accept it. It is its own spirit form, so it may take only what it needs. Allow yourself to be the reflector of the spirit form of the plant or animal.

When you are through, disengage and give thanks. Thank all the beings of Earth and Sky, the Earthly Mother and all beings of light. Thank them for returning all energy and debris that does not belong to its rightful place where it does belong and sustaining the healing influence.

Using a Kachina for Distance Healing

In healing from afar, it's often useful to use an object to represent the plant or animal being treated. It's not required, but it helps us to focus our intent. For example, in healing an animal, you could use a teddy bear, or a crafted dummy of some kind. I use one that was made for me; it looks like a large white sock filled with stuffing, which I've drawn a smiling face upon. Some medicine men use figures they have crafted, which some call a kachina, to either be the person, plant or animal in need of healing, or to represent spirit helpers or Powers that they will arrange around the object representing the patient. "Kachina" is a Hopi word meaning "super-natural being," referring to specific spirits, but it also refers to a carved doll that may represent the being. The carved objects, whether ornate or simply showing rough features, are merely to keep the mind focused on the ceremony at hand, so whatever fits your fancy is fine. Popsicle sticks will do. But once made, they can be carried in your medicine bag or kept at home for use again and again. To heal at a distance using a kachina, create your sacred circle, and with you sitting in the East, place the object for the plant or animal in the center and kachinas representing spirits of Earth and Sky, if you wish, arrayed around it. Hold your hands on either side of the object and connect with the Powers in your Crazy 8s, stretching your butterfly wings.

Healing By Raising Vibration Rate

For healing plants and animals through raising vibration rate at a distance, simply "check in" using kinesiology, as was discussed with the work of David R. Hawkins in Chapter 2, along with the simple yes/no practice exercise.

First, ask: May I access all that I Am at this time? And check in.

Then, ask: May I connect with all beings of light to assist me? Then check in.

Next, ask: May I perform healing for the highest good? Then check in.

The process of checking in itself raises your vibration rate. So, if you get a "no," simply breathe slowly, in and out from your diaphragm and allow all stresses to leave your body and mind, releasing them to the Universe and all beings. Clear your mind, finding the Stillpoint. Try again. You may wish to review Exercises 3, 4, 5 and 6. When you receive yeses to all the questions, ask: May I connect with (the plant or animal) for healing, health and wholeness? Then, check in. See what comes to mind: thoughts, feelings, impressions. As each arises, say: I acknowledge and release this, it is good.

You may be amazed at what comes forward, but don't attach to anything that arises into consciousness. Simply repeat with each instance: I acknowledge and release this, it is good. You will feel the shift when the session is over. When you feel this shift, simply say: Thank you, Creator, for allowing this moment. Please remove any energies that do not belong to me or (the plant or animal) and return them where they belong.[2]

Healing Plants and Animals at Interface or Mirroring

Plants and animals may be healed in proximity or at a distance by simply doing nothing. If consciously doing nothing sounds startling, it's called being at interface or mirroring. We constantly mirror our surroundings, energetically affecting all within our 27-foot energy field, whether human, plant or animal, and they affect us. Since every being has an energy field, every being is constantly blending, channeling and mirroring; interacting when they are together and through their multidimensional selves at a distance. To use this fact of relationship as a healing method, one can simply withdraw one's energy field so that one is consciously not sending energy (channeling) or sharing or taking on energy.

Learning to be at interface is learning to feel how your energy body operates. To do this, take a living object — such as a plant or a friend, relative or loved one — and sit across from each other. If the other is a plant, you don't have to ask it anything, except thank it for being there, but if it's a person, ask him or her to simply sit and be, with no thoughts, just being consciously present. Ask the person to close his or her eyes, if that helps them to be present. Now, hold your hands in front of you, palms out, and close your eyes. Feel your energy body. Feel how far out it extends in time and space. It seems limitless, doesn't it? Now, define your energy by the energy body of the person or plant sitting across from you. If you are using your hands instead of your mind: imagine your hands meeting the hands of the one sitting across from you; if it's a plant, imagine it has hands. Now feel where your energy meets that energy, as if your hands were pressing against the other's hands, neither pushing the other, just the defining point of interface.[3] When you imagine it this way, it becomes apparent where one's energy begins and another's leaves off. Now imagine that your energy field is a multitude of mirrors and that these mirrors are reflecting back the other's energy field. Allow yourself to be totally present — no thoughts — just being. This "doing nothing" is actually healing: allowing the other to "see" itself. If you are a perfect mirror feeling from your heart, being content, being only "present" with no angry or urgent thoughts, or thinking about yesterday or tomorrow, then the other will see of itself what it needs to see in order to find its own healing, harmony and balance.

One can apply this exercise to plants and animals at a distance by simply placing one's intent on mirroring that plant or animal. Since we are all connected across time and space, the intent will connect with the other's inherent wisdom and it will see what it needs to see. Make sure when you are finished that you thank Creator and ask that all energy that doesn't belong to you or the other person is removed and returned where it belongs.

Healing at a Distance Using Crystals

Healing a plant or animal at a distance can be accomplished using a crystal and a tripod. Any crystal will do. It doesn't have to be large or clear; in fact, it's a misconception that clear quartz crystals are in any way more "powerful" than smoky or milky ones, and small crystals (one inch or less) are plenty powerful. Clear crystals are called "museum" quality because that's what's desired for aesthetic reasons; it has nothing to do with utility, or their ability to hold or transmit energy. Most of the crystals I use for healing long distance are about 1–2 inches long and about one half-inch wide.

First, make a tripod by wrapping three sticks together at one end with string. Next, tie on a crystal so that it hangs down at the center of the tripod. Then fashion a doll or other item to represent the plant or animal needing healing, or in the case of a pet, write the animal's name on a piece of paper and place it under the tripod. Program the crystal by holding it in your left hand and feeling the energy from your heart flowing into it. Leave the tripod and crystal up to effect time-release healing, reprogramming the crystal occasionally. Such healing action can go on for days or weeks, if needed.

Healing at a Distance with Crystals Using Symbols

If for any reason a tripod is unwieldy, healing at a distance using crystals can also be done in the following alternative way. On the ground or on a piece of paper, draw the tesseract, umane or antahkarana symbols. Draw a circle around the symbols to contain and focus the energy in the space. Place the doll or piece of paper containing the animal's name in the circle and program four crystals with heart energy. Place a crystal at each corner of the symbol so that the crystal's tip is within the circle. The crystals with tips placed within the circle act as bridges between earth and sky for healing. You can also use the symbols with a tripod. Further, since the energy of the Umane is that of the Earth Mother, you can increase the power of the ceremony by making the Umane of Earth in the following way: dig a small square with corners stretching out like triangles, about one inch into the earth, or beneath the level of vegetation. Encircle the umane symbol with sun-bleached sand, or earth that has been dried in the sun, or with gifts to the Powers such as cornmeal or tobacco.

Using Other Healing Stones

In healing plants and animals at a distance, one may wish to employ healing stones. Stones have their unique vibrations and some help with one thing more than another. They are natural channels of energy. When put together, they act like a piano's keys playing a tune according to how they are selected and arranged.

Put another way: each of the Creator's stones has a vibration; each has an affinity for one thing or another. When put together, they create a harmony or overtone that can help keep you in harmony with the intent you want to achieve.

Remember intent is everything. We give energy by attention, where we put our focus, our energy. We achieve or bring things into reality by intention. Of course, mixed in there are male and female properties. So-called female properties attract, like magnetism; male energies direct. If properly chosen, stones are power objects that can have great effect in proximity or at a distance.

For thousands of years, Cherokee medicine men, or priests, have carried crystals with them for healing and other uses. Some people today mistakenly attribute crystal use to New Age thought, but it's indigenous. Among some tribes in the West, medicine men are leery of people who carry crystals. They wonder why someone would want to carry such a powerful stone. They are right, in a sense. Sometimes, especially on the road when doing Drum Circle, I'll pick up the stones in the parking lot of wherever we may be. Just whatever stones call to me. They have power, too. They are grandfathers, like the mightiest of boulders. Their wisdom is old. It doesn't matter that they were found in a parking lot. Power is anywhere and everywhere.

Crystals are the most recognizable of stones that have Power because they are pretty and popular. They magnify energy but they're not very choosy. All stones have personalities, if you will. Crystals are happy-go-lucky — sort of like puppy dogs — but some can be dangerous. You usually don't see those in rock shops or hanging around people's necks. Nonetheless, a stone shaman — someone who understands the properties, vibrations and healing abilities of stones — can use them to affect various intents. Dangerous crystals are not dangerous in themselves, in that crystals only magnify energy; but a dangerous crystal would be one that could focus energy in such a way as to cause damage through pointing, for example. In the hands of someone with bad intent, pointing a crystal with sharp focusing ability at someone could cause harm. It is best to treat crystals as powerful stones worthy of respect, with good intent.

You may remember that in the Old Testament (Exodus 28:17–20), a breastplate was described that had great power: 'Set it with four rows of mounted stones. The first of these rows shall contain a ruby, an emerald and a crystal. The second row: carbuncle, sapphire, pearl. The third row: topaz, turquoise, calf eye. The fourth row: chrysolite, onyx, jasper.' These stones, it was said, were placed in their fullness in gold settings. After the breastplate was woven and folded over, it was set with four rows of precious stones: ruby, emerald, crystal; carbuncle, sapphire, pearl; topaz, turquoise calf eye; chrysolite, onyx, jasper. The four rows paralleled the four directions. Funny, how all the ancient teachings of indigenous peoples all over the world tell similar stories and offer similar ways. The breastplate was not only a healing garment that would help the healer and the healed, but it channeled Power from above, to give insight, direction and bring out the best qualities of each of the tribes of Israel. Each tribe had its stone (vibration) that, unfortunately, has been corrupted today into the idea of birthstones.

The garment can be seen as a medicine wheel. We do the same when we drum, calling in the four directions. When the stones are used in this way, in sacred geometry, they are being used to magnify the star tetrahedron that is the energy body. The wearer is connected in time and space to all things, all events — a merkaba. Sometimes medicine men will grind stones into powder to make "paint." In cowboy movies, the war paint is a mainstay, but it's a bit more complicated than that. Paint is actually medicine, because of the power that the stones convey. This paint can be used in ceremony for healing, but one must be very careful, as some stones have toxic qualities that can be harmful if breathed or absorbed through the skin. Moreover, ground herbs can be mixed with the stone powder for healing qualities. This paint can be used on the plant or animal to be treated, on the kachina or as part of a gifting to the Powers in ceremony.

When using stones for healing, speak with the stones as you would with plants and animals — in meditation, drumming or shamanic journey — to find which ones offer to be used and select them accordingly. Arrange the stones in the sacred circle around that which you are treating. Their vibration will help effect healing according to the attributes they have to offer and the effect or vibration that is needed.[4]

Soul Retrieval of Plants and Animals

Using a rattle to retrieve lost soul pieces is one of the easiest and most powerful ceremonies one can do alone. Often, when people think of rattling or performing sacred ceremony of any kind, they may think it requires any number of people participating. Actually, whenever anyone does sacred ceremony, many are participating: Creator, guides, spirits, Earth Mother, ancestors and spirits of the land. A whole host of beings are present whenever prayers and ceremony are performed; the number of people in bodies is inconsequential to the ceremony itself, though it's a great blessing to share ceremonies with others.

Retrieving lost soul pieces is a powerful ceremony in itself.[5]

Whenever trauma occurs, the injury causes a piece of soul essence to be ejected. For example, just before a car crash the driver's consciousness does not want to be present when the person's body collides with the steering wheel, so a piece is ejected at the moment of impact. It is the role of the shaman to go out into non-ordinary reality and retrieve the lost piece. In ancient times, indigenous people understood this and whenever people experienced trauma, they were treated immediately for soul loss. When warriors came back from battle, they would avoid contact with the villagers until ceremonies had been held to cleanse them from the bloodshed and retrieve soul pieces lost due to the trauma of war. Soul loss can be experienced for many other reasons as well, such as bad relationships, death of a relationship or loved one, divorce, child abuse or drug or alcohol abuse, even if the precipitating event occurred decades before.

Symptoms of soul loss include loss of life force, feeling apart from life, feeling depressed or suicidal, being prone to addiction, post-traumatic stress syndrome, excessive grief or a deep sense that something is missing. The best way to retrieve soul pieces is for a trained practitioner to bring them back, though often such pieces return on their own and hover around the person. In my practice of soul retrieval, I've frequently found that when people start looking for someone to retrieve missing soul pieces, it means some of them have already returned. Since lost pieces are often linked, it may take only a little effort and knowledge to get all the remaining pieces to come back, usually by rattling. But this can also be applied to plants and animals. Any type of rattle will do; it doesn't have to be ornate or special. A child's rattle is fine and a makeshift rattle can be made by using an empty plastic drink bottle with a few pebbles in it, or even a bottle of aspirin in a pinch (though the aspirin probably won't fare well).

To perform soul retrieval by rattling, first create a sacred circle, preferably in a secluded place in nature. Ask

Ask

your guides, angels, and power animals to aid you. Thank them through affirmation for doing so. Next clear your mind, finding your Stillpoint, open yourself, trusting that you are protected, then begin rattling with the intent of calling in missing soul pieces of the plant or animal. You may experience odd emotions or have unusual insights. Don't push them away or analyze them, but simply allow the memories to come into consciousness, acknowledge them and let them go. This is the energy of the being you are treating interacting with your energy field; you are a witness here, allowing the missing soul parts to reseat themselves.

Once the rattling is complete, simply let the soul pieces reestablish themselves. By that I mean, when you are through rattling, give the plant or animal your conscious intent of "allowing." Allow a moment of peace to descend. Allow a moment of settling or a moment of silence, if that is how you wish to perceive it. Soul pieces will find their places while you are watching and after you are gone. But if you give a moment of conscious intent to allow things to come together, it aids the process. When finished, clear yourself, giving the affirmation of returning all energetic debris where it belongs.

Learning the Song of the Plant or Animal

As we have seen, raising our own vibration rate allows us and all living things to heal and even draws divine powers to connect with the land. By raising our vibration rate, we are drawn to powerful places, as well, and plants and animals will draw themselves to us. As David R. Hawkins explains, in the high 500s of vibration rate, everything begins to happen by synchronicity, and the events of life unfold in perfect order and harmony with precise timing.[6] With this high vibration rate, we may wish to learn the unique song of a plant or animal. This can be done through drumming, which raises vibration rate; through shamanic journey, which allows our spirit form to travel and see and hear; or through meditation, practicing our Crazy 8s. The song of a plant or animal is its own unique signature frequency as a species, with only minute differences for the individual. Special sacred plants, such as peyote, may teach many songs because they have a larger consciousness that connects to many things such as doorways between worlds. To learn a plant or animal's song, simply listen with your heart, practicing the heyoka remembering. What tune comes forward? It may seem a rather mindless melody. Sometimes the animals in the forest may help us, to draw attention to a plant that may need to teach us something. The bird may even mimic the song of the plant. By learning the animal or plant's song, not only are you allowing this plant or animal to help heal you (and other beings where this frequency and encoded knowledge is needed) but by singing it back to the plant or animal, you are also helping to heal it by reinforcing its spirit form with your added energy. It's worth noting that no plant or animal attacks itself. If you learn the song of the plant or animal, you will be immune from harm from it. For example, mosquitoes have their own song, which is close to the sound they make when flying; if you learn the mosquito's song, no mosquito will bite you. They may hover around you, enjoying the song, but will not light. A good way to learn the songs of plants or animals is to go into the forest where there are few human noises, create a sacred circle and drum or meditate until a song begins to emerge. You will find that the song belongs to a particular plant or animal that may be needed by you or for someone you love in your particular life situation to give healing or wisdom. Repeat the song and the plant or animal that produced it will appear more luminous than other plants and animals in the surroundings. The need for the song, the niche that it fills in your life, will become apparent and the song can later be used when similar circumstances present themselves, for yourself or others.

Being Peacemakers among the Nations

Now that you have an introduction into holding dialogue with plants and animals, it is up to you to practice what you have learned, and that includes your way of being. To learn to be is probably the most critical lesson; it is to be at peace with ourselves, so we bring peace to the world.

To do this work, we appreciate the power of peace, of having enough, of knowing that at any moment Creator gives us everything we need. It is humorous that as I'm writing this, a best-selling book called *The Secret,* is making the rounds with the premise that the Law of Attraction will give us everything we need.[7] The Law of Attraction is very real and it's no secret that it works. But the secret — **THE** secret — is not that if we think positive thoughts of abundance that abundance will be ours, but that abundance is all around us all the time and it is an active principle.

We always have enough. We are always praying, not just on Sundays or days or hours set aside, and our prayers are always answered. We must only recognize what we are praying for (using the Law of Attraction to bring) and recognize when it's before us.

If we think we need more than what Creator gives us, then think again. What is awry? Perhaps it is the think part. Think again. Has Creator not given us everything we need upon this great, green Earth, this mother who provides all life? What is it that we think we need to acquire that we do not already have or already know? Do we not have all the tools at our disposal to give us what we need? This is the way of peace. Not reacting, not wanting, not acquiring, but being grateful for all that is given to us and seeing the abundance all around us. If we think we need more than we have, then we are not seeing the abundance that is given. Allow, accept, acknowledge and be grateful. That is the way of peace, the way of abundance. We will never want if we recognize that we always have exactly what we need. That is The Secret. If we use the Law of Attraction to try to bring what we want, we'll always have want. And what is trying but an excuse for not doing? If you try to eat or drink, you will by definition fail; if you eat or drink, then the action is performed.

Peace is not an inactive principle; it is not acceptance or acquiescence. It is not passive or inert. Peace is a way of being, an active principle. It is an active form of respect. As I've mentioned, among Native peoples the greatest sin is to be rude. Among traditional Native Americans, the principle of respect extends beyond the immediate to all beings in the world. Many young people have forgotten this today and it is a sad thing. When a young person, or even an adult, acts in a rude manner, being loud, demanding or accusing, a traditional person is often embarrassed — not by the anger, demands or accusations, but for the person making them, because it shows a lack of respect for life itself and all beings. Such rudeness is often met with silence — not out of anger, or rejection, but out of respect for self, for the person who shows such lack of self-respect. Unfortunately, among many people today, rudeness is seen as strength. It is not. It is weakness. Peace, with its attendant quality of patience, is true strength. The basis of that strength is Power... Creator's power.

Creator is all powerful, but Creator doesn't show power through anger or displays of destruction. Natural destruction upon the Earth is always to make way for more and better: more life, more diversity, more creation. That is the way of peace; it breaks down, but it builds up. It is a process that always takes in that which was and transmutes it so that it can be something that creates better. The Earth, with Creator, always walks in balance and beauty, and this is the path toward survival: survival of the world, survival of species, survival of the Earth herself. The secret to survival of all beings, the greatest secret upon the Earth and the most powerful, is respect. The respect that we give to all beings, the plant and animal nations, the various peoples of the Earth and all beings, in harmony, is the force of sacredness that extends generation upon generation. When we hold up one of our hands, we see this, with four fingers and the thumb. The thumb is our unique, individual self; the four fingers are the balance of our relations, mother, father, grandmother, grandfather. We hold our hands out in friendship, each one of us as members of the five-fingered tribe, one people, all colors, giving balance to all that we find with these our healing hands.

When we walk in balance, as Children of Earth and Sky, we are regaining our rightful place in the world, being in right relationship with all the other beings of the Earth. When we act, not out of selfishness, but in sharing and applying what we know so that all may be healed and in balance, we are healing the Earth and ourselves. This is the Sacred Hoop of Life, respecting ourselves for who we truly are and all beings for who they truly are. All our relations, all of us dependent upon the other to keep the circle from being broken. Each point on this circle, each being — ourselves, rocks, trees, plants, birds — has its place in the circle. There is no above or below, better or less, all are equal in keeping the Sacred Circle of Life, this world in which we live, alive, in balance, in the process of peace that is Creator creating. And this role extends through time, from our ancestors to our selves to our children and our children's children — in Native way, for seven generations yet to come. Our bodies are merely vehicles for spirit, as miraculous as they are; they depend upon the other physical attributes of the Earthly Mother to survive, in concert with every being. Sadly, as a culture, we are like unruly, rude children, uncaring in our stewardship of the plant and animal nations, and with the Earthly Mother herself. If we do not amend our ways and practice the peace that is the way of the world, coexisting in harmony and balance, our mother will greet our behavior with a silence so eternal that there will be no more Children of Earth and Sky.

It is our responsibility to ensure that does not happen. Our ancestors gave us the tools and examples of how to live in peace, harmony, balance and beauty. We give away nothing by following their footsteps as applied to the world today, except peace, harmony, healing and goodness. We each have a powerful role to play in ensuring that the wisdom of the ancestors is part of the Earth walk of those who follow us in generations yet to come. It is up to us now, as holders of our place, to do our part. We must return to right relationship. And do it now.

This book is offered as a path toward right relationship. It is now up to you to walk the path, if you see it as a good way to go. By bringing balance and harmony to ourselves and sharing it with the plant and animal nations, we bring healing to the world. What a wonderful gift to give and to receive: healing Earth and ourselves, fulfilling our soul purpose as Children of Earth and Sky.

Wisatologi Nihi! Many Blessings on your path.

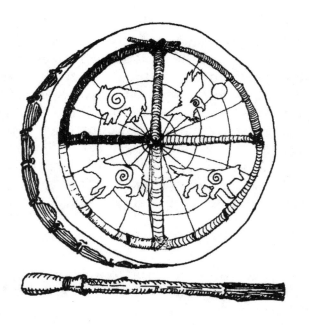

Notes

Preface

1. Japanese researcher Masaru Emoto has extensively documented the power of intent on changing the molecular makeup of water. See his book *The Message from Water,* vols. 1 and 2 (Tokyo, Japan: Hado Kyoikusha, 2004), or visit his Web site, at www.masaru-emoto.net. Also, for more on transmutation of substances and healing ceremonies for the Earth, see Sandra Ingerman's book, *Medicine for the Earth: How to Transform Personal and Environmental Toxins.* You may write to Ms. Ingerman to obtain a schedule of her 'Medicine for the Earth' workshops, at P.O. Box 4757, Santa Fe, NM 87502. Or visit her Web site at www.shamanicvisions.com.

2. See the book *1491: New Revelations of the Americas before Columbus* by Charles C. Mann (New York: Knopf, 2005).

3. Jane Brody, in *The New York* Times ("To Preserve Their Health and Heritage, Arizona Indians Reclaim Ancient Foods," May 12, 1991), writes: On the Arizona desert, the desirable food ingredients are found in edible parts of such indigenous plants as the mesquite (mes-KEET) tree, cholla (CHOY-a) and prickly pear cactus, as well as in tepary (TEP-a-ree) beans, chia (CHEE-a) seeds and acorns from live oaks. Tribal elders speak fondly of these one-time favorites, which in recent decades have been all but forgotten as hamburgers, fries, soft drinks and other fatty, sugary, overly refined fast and packaged foods gained favor. Even those Indians who still rely heavily on beans and corn are today consuming varieties that have little or none of the nutritive advantages found in the staples of their historic diet. For example, the sweet corn familiar to Americans contains rapidly digested starches and sugars, which raise sugar levels in the blood, while the hominy-type corn of

the traditional Indian diet has little sugar and mostly starch that is slowly digested.

Similarly, the pinto beans that the federal government now gives to the Indians (along with lard, refined wheat flour, sugar, coffee and processed cereals) are far more rapidly digested than the tepary beans the Tohon O'odham once depended upon. Indeed, their former tribal name is a distorted version of the Indian word meaning "the Bean People." When Earl Ray, a Pima Indian who lives near Phoenix, switched to a more traditional native diet of mesquite meal, tepary beans, cholla buds and chaparral tea, he dropped from 239 pounds to less than 150 and brought his severe diabetes under control without medication. In a federally financed study of 11 Indian volunteers predisposed to diabetes, a diet of native foods rich in fiber and complex carbohydrates kept blood sugar levels on an even keel and increased the effectiveness of insulin. When switched back to a low-fiber "convenience-market diet" containing the same number of calories, the volunteers' blood sugar skyrocketed and their sensitivity to insulin declined.

An excellent source for native foods and their sources is NATIVE SEEDS/S.E.A.R.C.H., a non-profit organization that seeks to preserve the crop seeds that connect Native American cultures to their land. Through seed conservation and community interaction Native Seeds/SEARCH works to protect crop biodiversity and celebrate cultural diversity. See the Web site: www.nativeseeds.org/.

4. See note 2, preface, Mann, et al.

5. See the book by Edward O Wilson, *Biophilia: The Human Bond with Other Species*. Boston: Harvard University Press, 1986.

6. Volume 20 No. 3, the April 2001 issue of the *American Journal of Preventive Medicine*. Frumkin compiled research that suggests people can benefit from distinct types of

encounters with nature: contact with animals, plants, natural landscapes and the wilderness. One study, for example, showed that prisoners whose cells faced a prison courtyard made about 25 percent more sick visits than did those who had a view of farmland. The same has held true for people whose hospital rooms have a window. People who have pets have lower blood pressure and cholesterol levels than non-pet owners, according to another study Frumkin mentions. Examples include lower blood pressure, improved survival after heart attacks and enhanced ability to cope with stress. Contact with plants, from gardening to looking at trees, could also contribute to healing physical and mental ailments, he asserts. For example, office employees report that simply having plants in the workplace makes them feel calmer. This may be the basis of traditional healing gardens in hospitals, and of the horticultural therapy that is now widely used in acute hospitals, children's hospitals, nursing homes, psychiatric hospitals and hospices. Evolution may have hard-wired humans with a preference for specific natural settings. "Early humans found that places with open views offered better opportunities to find food and avoid predators," he explains. See other works on biophilia by Stephen Kellert and Lynn Margulis. The opposite is biophobia, which is being averse to the natural world.

7. It was our great honor to be invited to perform Medicine Wheel Ceremony in 2005 for the Earth Ethics Institute in Miami, Fla., one of many organizations that support and encourage right relationship between farming/food practices and Earth. Since 1993, the Earth Ethics Institute has been a catalyst for introducing administrators, faculty, staff and students at Miami Dade College to a new way of thinking called "Earth Literacy" that fosters respect for the Earth and life in all its diversity. Earth Ethics Institute provides resources, workshops, and programs for the Miami Dade College community, the largest community college in the nation, fostering an awareness of global

interdependence, ecological integrity through biological diversity and the natural processes that sustain life aimed at promoting these values in the South Florida community and the extended Earth community beyond. For more information, see: www.earthethicsinstitute.org.

8. Boyd, Doug. *Mad Bear: Spirit, Healing, and the Sacred in the Life of a Native American Medicine Man.* New York: Touchstone, 1994.

Chapter One

1. See *USA Today,* March 16, 2006, "Big Bang unfolded in the blink of an eye."

2. For more on the "medicine wheel" and ceremonies that can be performed using the medicine wheel, including those of your own devising, see my book *Finding Sanctuary in Nature: Simple Ceremonies in the Native American Tradition for Healing Yourself and Others,* illustrated by Annette Waya Ewing. (Findhorn, Scotland: Findhorn Press, 2007)

3. For more on DNA, see: International Chimpanzee Chromosome 22 Consortium, "DNA sequence and comparative analysis of chimpanzee chromosome 22," *Nature,* 429:382–388, May 27, 2004.

4. For more on consecrating spaces and enlisting the aid of the Powers, see my book, *Clearing: A Guide for Liberating Energies Trapped in Buildings and Lands,* illustrated by Annette Waya Ewing, with a foreword by Brooke Medicine Eagle (Findhorn, Scotland: Findhorn Press, 2006).

5. This exercise is included in my book, *Finding Sanctuary in Nature: Simple Ceremonies in the Native American Tradition for Healing Yourself and Others.* You will notice that the medicine wheel we use is composed of the four races of human beings, red, yellow, black and white; the colors vary among tribes and even within tribes, and also may vary for specific ceremonies employing a medicine wheel.

6. This way of seeing — dividing the world into the *tonal* and *nagual* — is amply outlined in other books on the Toltec way of shamanism. For more information, see the books by Carlos Castaneda, such as *The Teachings of Don Juan: A Yaqui Way of Knowledge*. New York: Ballantine, 1969, Don Mguel Ruiz, such as *The Four Agreements*. San Rafael, Calif.: Amber-Allen Publishing, 1997, and Ken Eagle Feather's *A Toltec Path*. Charlottesville, Va.: Hampton Roads, 1995. Approaching reality from this perspective, because of the popularity of these teachings, has become a form of consensus reality that readily embraces non-ordinary reality, or the shamanic way of viewing the world, and, hence, is easily translatable into shifting our way of perceiving the world.

7. See Drunvalo Melchizedek's books *Ancient Secrets of the Flower of Life,* vols. 1 and 2 (Flagstaff, AZ: Light Technology Publishing, 1990), which are taught in courses given by Flower of Life Research LLC, P.O. Box 55844, Phoenix, AZ 85078; phone: 602-996-0900; Web site: www.floweroflife.org. The books and courses are both highly recommended.

Chapter Two

1. There are several versions of these stories; see Indigenous Peoples Literature, www.indigenouspeople.net/.

2. For more stories about Coyote, see: *Coyote Stories* by Mourning Dove (Lincoln and London, Neb: University of Nebraska Press, 1990); also, see Jamie Sams, *Dancing the Dream: The Seven Sacred Paths of Human Transformation* (New York: HarperCollins, 1998) and Christopher Moore, *Coyote Blue* (New York: HarperCollins, 2004). Sams's book gives excellent teachings on the medicine wheel, including how Coyote comes in to mess up our plans and ideas. Moore's book is about having Coyote as a power animal, or spirit guide, and the types of tricks he plays.

3. Although the Native American Church, which I attend from time to time, regards the sacred plant peyote as a powerful sacrament, it is not necessary to take medicine of any kind to dialogue with — or heal — plants and animals.

4. Some very handy books on finding herbs and medicinal plants are the Peterson Field Guides, including *A Field Guide to Medicinal Plants and Herbs: Eastern and Central North America* (Boston: Houghton Mifflin Company, 1999) and *A Field Guide to Edible Wild Plants: Eastern and Central North America* (Boston: Houghton Mifflin Company, 1999).

5. This technique, called the Gassho Meditation, is taught by William Lee Rand, founder of the International Center for Reiki Training. For more information about Reiki, including books and workshops teaching Reiki, contact the International Center for Reiki Training, 21421 Hilltop Street, Unit #28, Southfield, MI 48034. Phone: 800-332-8112. Web site: www.reiki.org.

6. For millennia, Native Americans have practiced various ceremonies for learning to connect with the authentic self through the pipe fast, or vision quest. For more, see my book: *Finding Sanctuary in Nature: Simple Ceremonies in the Native American Tradition for Healing Yourself and Others,* illustrated by Annette Waya Ewing (Findhorn, Scotland: Findhorn Press, 2007)

7. See the book *Through the Looking-Glass* by Lewis Carroll. Austin, Texas: 1st World Library, 2004.

8. For more on the energy field, see Note 7, Chapter 1, regarding Drunvalo Melchizedek, sacred geometry; various exercises expanding this knowledge can be learned in the Flower of Life courses.

9. This barrage of energy is why I don't live in — or even like to visit — large cities. It takes too much energy to shield, depleting me and making me irritable. If I lived in a large city (and I lived for a while in New York City), constantly

grounding and shielding can become a habit, so it's not so onerous. But I prefer as remote a region as possible to allow my energy body to stretch out and soar. Once the door of perception is opened, it's imperative that we practice discernment of energy and stay grounded, centered and shielded, no matter where we are.

10. Lest you think being able to "tune in" to people's energy is an asset, it generally is not. People are a constantly bubbling cauldron of thought fragments and shifting emotions.

11. For more on animal totems and the energy of animals, see the wonderful books by Ted Andrews, such as *Animal Speak: The Spiritual and Magical Powers of Creatures Great and Small* (St. Paul, Minn: Llewellyn Publications, 1998) and *Animal-Wise: The Spirit Language and Signs of Nature* (St. Paul, Minn: Llewellyn Publications, 1999).

12. For more examples of the Fourth Dimension, see the book by Rudolf Steiner, *The Fourth Dimension: Sacred Geometry, Alchemy, and Mathematics,* Great Barrington, Mass.: Anthroposophic Press, 2001.

13. See The Projection of Fourfold Figures upon a Three-Flat by T. Proctor Hall, *American Journal of Mathematics,* Vol. 15, No. 2, April 1893.

14. See the book by Rupert Sheldrake, *A New Science of Life,* Los Angeles: JP Tarcher, 1982.

15. Energies enter a given space through specific angles, which the circle is designed to limit unless they are invited. For more on this, see my books: *Clearing: A Guide for Liberating Energies Trapped in Buildings and Lands*, illustrated by Annette Waya Ewing, with a foreword by Brooke Medicine Eagle (Findhorn, Scotland: Findhorn Press, 2006) and *Finding Sanctuary in Nature: Simple Ceremonies in the Native American Tradition for Healing Yourself and Others.*

16. Each shape has its own energy, as part of its sacred geometry. For example, the sphere represents void, the

tetrahedron fire, the hexahedron earth, the octahedron air, the icosahedron water, the dodecahedron ether or prana; each has a healing power by bringing harmony to whatever is placed within their energetic framework, bringing higher vibrations to bear. A number of Native American symbols have Power and are universal; for example, Golden Eagle, formerly known as Standing Elk, a member of the Dakota Ihunktowan Band of South Dakota, a spiritual elder, and one of the seven Sundance Chiefs of the Yankton Sioux, has co-authored the book *Maka Wicahpi Wicohan,* available along with symbols and explanations on his Web site: www.star-knowledge.net/. Here in Lena, we often use The Alphabet of the Star Beings (Dolphins and Whales) for ceremonies because the symbols of the alphabet themselves have power. For more information, see the Web site: Healing The Earth/ Ourselves, www.blueskywaters.com.

17. You may order symbols from our webpage, and the International Center for Reiki Training offers a downloadable version of the Antahkarana through its Web site: www.reiki.org.

18. See the book by Richard Gerber, M.D., *Vibrational Medicine: New Choices for Healing Ourselves.* Santa Fe, N.M.: Bear and Company, 1996.

19. See the book *Secret Life of Plants* by Chris Bird and Peter Tompkins, New York: Harper Paperbacks, 1989.

20. See the book *Primary Perception: Biocommunication with Plants, Living Foods, and Human Cells* by Cleve Backster, Anza, Calif.: White Rose Millennium Press, 2003.

21. For more on healing ceremonies, see my previous book *Finding Sanctuary in Nature: Simple Ceremonies in the Native American Tradition for Healing Yourself and Others.*

22. For working with divine beings in clearing spaces, and removing negative vibrations, see by previous book: *Clearing: A Guide for Liberating Energies Trapped in Buildings and Lands.*

23. For more on dynamics of prayer, see my previous book *Finding Sanctuary in Nature: Simple Ceremonies in the Native American Tradition for Healing Yourself and Others.*

24. For more on creating sacred space, see my previous book: *Clearing: A Guide for Liberating Energies Trapped in Buildings and Lands.*

25. See the book *Power vs. Force: The Hidden Determinants of Human Behavior* by David R. Hawkins, M.D., Ph.D., Carlsbad, Calif.: Hay House, 1995.

26. This and similar exercises were taught by the late Debra Harrison, who with Dr. Mary A. Lynch formed a wellness model through Consegrity, Inc., that is no longer in business. The wellness model, however, continues as Consilience; see www.energymirrors.com.

27. For more, see Wayne W. Dyer's book *The Power of Intention,* Carlsbad, Calif.: Hay House, 2004.

28. For more on Reiki, see Note 5.

29. Although this method of handling energy through reflection was taught by the now gone wellness model of Consegrity®, and its successor, consilience, my problem with this technique as taught is that it disavows Spirit, relying on mental gymnastics, so that the rules of practicing it are constantly changing to keep the practitioners in the right frame of mind. It's too left-brained. If it were based on Spirit, the constantly shifting techniques to satisfy the left-brain's rationality wouldn't be necessary, nor would the massive amounts of printed material required to practice it be necessary. For a while, I practiced this modality as part of my medicine bag, but quickly discovered through working with Native peoples that it was counterproductive. It requires that a huge tome of written mirrors and explanatory material hundreds of page in length be used and when I carried that into the person's home, their suspicions were aroused. In their eyes, the only people who carry such massive documentation

were lawyers and government officials, neither of which they desired in an hour of need.

30. For more about Reiki, see our Web page: Healing The Earth/Ourselves www.blueskywaters.com or Note 5.

Chapter Three

1. The Foundation for Shamanic Studies teaches how to journey in its workshops. For more information, contact the Foundation for Shamanic Studies, P.O. Box 1939, Mill Valley, CA 94942. Phone: 415-380-8282. Web site: www.shamanism.org

   Also, see Alberto Villoldo's Four Winds Society at www.thefourwinds.org. Also, see Sandra Ingerman's book, *Shamanic Journeying: A Beginner's Guide* (Boulder, CO: Sounds True, 2004), which includes a drumming CD and simple instructions.

2. We offer CDs to aid in journeying on our Web site, Healing the Earth/Ourselves, www.blueskywaters.com, as does the Foundation, www.shamanism.org.

3. For more on how to connect with spirits, consecrate/clear lands and promote healing through ceremony, see my previous books *Clearing: A Guide for Liberating Energies Trapped in Buildings and Lands,* illustrated by Annette Waya Ewing, with a foreword by Brooke Medicine Eagle (Findhorn, Scotland: Findhorn Press, 2006) and *Finding Sanctuary in Nature: Simple Ceremonies in the Native American Tradition for Healing Yourself and Others,* illustrated by Annette Waya Ewing, with a foreword by Ven. Chief Dhyani Ywahoo (Findhorn, Scotland: Findhorn Press, 2007).

4. There are two chemicals that may help, if one has difficulty, but check with your doctor first, if you find that you may need them, to ensure it is OK. Both are herbal dietary supplements. The first is melatonin, which has the effect of stimulating dreams, making them more visual. If

needed, use the 3 mg as recommended on the label as a dietary supplement, but make sure you do not purchase the time-release formula. Take before bedtime; but be apprised, you may dream so much that you don't get a restful night's sleep. This stimulation of the area of the brain for dreaming can help if you are also learning to journey as it provides a natural pathway for seeing. It helps to promote journeying also if you practice remembering your dreams when you awaken (whether taking melatonin or not) and keeping a dream journal for recording your dreams daily. I've kept a dream journal for years and many of the dreams have proved prophetic and also have offered great wisdom. As stated, for many years, all my shamanic work was done in Dreamtime, and indigenous people around the world have done so for millennia. Shamanic journey using the drum is a way of turning it on and off at will; so that you can journey at any time for any purpose for instant results, though the information or knowledge given to us by our guides and power animals may not be as we expect.

The other chemical is potassium. Doing energy work burns potassium at a high rate and can deplete the body of its reserves. Sometimes, a person has difficulty journeying because there is too little potassium in the body. When anticipating doing a lot of journeying, or ceremony, I'll take a 550 mg potassium gluconate tablet beforehand. Again, check with your physician to ensure that this vitamin supplement is safe for you, as people with heart conditions and high blood pressure and some other conditions may find it inappropriate. Potassium in high levels is also found in most sports drinks and naturally in bananas. One 550 mg pill equals one banana.

The herb Gingko can also help, for clarity, especially when taken in conjunction with St. John's Wort, which also acts as an anti-depressant; but they often have the side effect of weight loss. Some people cannot take these herbal supplements, so check with a doctor. I offer this information not to suggest they should be followed, but only as information if anyone is having difficulty journeying, as these are the only impediments I have found for people, out of hundreds taught. If you cannot take supplements of any kind, work on nighttime dreaming, and keeping a journal; this will exercise your brain, allowing the pathways to open up into waking consciousness.

5. See the book by Carlos Castaneda *Journey To Ixtlan: The Lessons of Don Juan.* New York: Simon and Schuster, 1977.

6. For more on the Christ Consciousness Grid and Plume of Quetzalcoatl, see my previous books: *Clearing: A Guide for Liberating Energies Trapped in Buildings and Lands and Finding Sanctuary in Nature: Simple Ceremonies in the Native American Tradition for Healing Yourself and Others.*

    For more on the Akashic field, see: *Science and the Akashic Field: An Integral Theory of Everything* by Ervin Laszlo, Rochester, Vt. : Inner Traditions, 2004.

7. This permeable layer, energetically, is the portion of the Earth Mother that we access to bring a place to its highest vibration point, or to bring ourselves up to our highest potential. Some call it the Christ Consciousness Grid, since it actually can be described as a grid upon the Earth, roughly corresponding with ley lines that cover the Earth like meridians of energy in acupuncture; but many Native people have a problem with Christ describing a holy place or energy, given the subjugation of Native peoples by foreign missionaries. Among medicine men, this energetic layer is often called The Plume of Quetzalcoatl. Among Western mystics, and in metaphysical literature, this layer is referred to as the Akashic Field.

8. Carroll, Note 7, Chapter 2.

9. This is the prescribed manner that is taught by the Foundation for Shamanic Studies, see Note 1; also, see the book by Michael Harner, founder of the Foundation for

Shamanic Studies, who conducted pioneering work in the effects of drumming that he then outlined in his book *The Way of the Shaman* (New York: Harper, 1980).

10. See Harner, Note 9.

11. For instruction in how to clear "ghosts," or energy fragments, entities or other unwanted energies from your house, or any space, see my previous book: *Clearing: A Guide for Liberating Energies Trapped in Buildings and Lands.*

Chapter Four

1. For more on the sacred geometry of land forms, see my previous book *Clearing: A Guide for Liberating Energies Trapped in Buildings and Lands,* illustrated by Annette Waya Ewing, with a foreword by Brooke Medicine Eagle (Findhorn, Scotland: Findhorn Press, 2006).

2. See Note 26, Chapter 2.

3. See Note 26, Chapter 2.

4. For more on uses of stones, see the book *Love Is in the Earth: A Kaleidoscope of Crystals* by Melody (Wheat Ridge, Colo.: Earth-Love Publishing House, Ltd, 1995); also for necklaces using healing stones, see our Web site Healing The Earth/Ourselves www.blueskywaters.com

5. To learn more about soul retrieval, see the book by Sandra Ingerman, *Soul Retrieval: Mending the Fragmented Self.* San Francisco: Harper, 1991. Sandra taught me soul retrieval and it's one of the mainstays of my practice. To learn more of Ingerman's courses and workshops, see Note 1, Preface; also, the Foundation for Shamanic Studies and Alberto Villoldo, Note 1, Chapter 3.

6. Hawkins, Note 25, Chapter 2.

7. *The Secret* Rhonda Byrne. New York: Simon and Schuster, 2006.

Glossary

allies. Wild spirits of the land that can aid in healing and protecting natural habitats.

all-time, no-time. The present, accessed at its deepest level.

angels. Emissaries of light of divine origin who accompany humans through life and are available for assistance and inspiration.

animus. The spark of life.

antahkarana. Ancient healing symbol, thousands of years old, which can be used for local and long-distance healing.

archetypes. Attributes existing in potential form that can be brought into manifestation; original models after which other similar things are patterned.

ascension. Transcending to a higher level of consciousness; the next step in human and planetary evolution.

aura. Emanations of the energy body, often seen as colors that show moods, thoughts or potentials; energetic fields surrounding the physical body, including physical, etheric, emotional, mental, astral, etheric template, celestial and causal.

authentic self. Who you really are, not who you think you are, or have been told you are by outside sources.

centering. Locating the core of consciousness in the body; drawing magnetic energy from the earth and electrical energy from the sun to operate with balanced awareness.

chakra. Sanskrit for circle or wheel; the energetic centers in the core of the body linked together by a central psychic energy channel.

Christ Consciousness Grid (also called the Plume of Quetzalcoatl). An energy layer surrounding the earth that signifies the earth's highest potential and that was supposedly established by higher beings, often referred to as ascended beings, to help humanity through the current "shift of the ages."

cleansing. Transmuting energy to a higher, more positive form by raising its vibrational rate.

clearing. Dissipating (transmuting) negative energy. Clearing spaces usually also cleanses them since the act of clearing raises the vibrational rate.

co-creating. Operating as a partner with the Creator to boost positive energy.

ego. The survival mechanism, which is part of the personality. See personality.

energy. Subtle power manifested through life force, frequency or cohesion.

energy body. A body that exists beyond the physical plane; in humans, such a body extends twenty-seven feet in each direction and thereafter continues into other dimensions. See aura.

fast. See vision quest.

fractal. A geometric pattern repeated at ever smaller scales to produce shapes and surfaces that cannot be represented by classical geometry but can recreate irregular patterns and structures in nature.

flow of creation. The movement or stasis of energy in a given moment.

God vs. Creator. God is one, all; the Creator is the active aspect of God as expressed in the will of creation.

goddesses. Land spirits of the highest order, usually associated with a place or characteristic; also, humans who have transcended but chosen to remain on earth in spirit form as a means of service.

grounding. Connecting with the earth energetically to ensure that consciousness is not operating from other dimensions or overly affected by other energetic forces.

guides. Spirit helpers, soul brothers or sisters from former or future lifetimes or spiritual masters who have assumed a supportive role for a particular soul's evolution.

heart song, or power song. A song that expresses the unique, positive energies, traits and intents of an individual, usually discovered through fasting and prayer.

higher power. God as expressed through one's highest nature.

kachinas. Supernatural beings revered by the Hopi and appearing as messengers from the spirit world; spirit beings; objects that may be crafted to represent the spirit body of beings.

lela wakan. Lakota term meaning "very sacred."

ley lines. Grids that crisscross the earth and hold potential electromagnetic energy, many of which were identified by ancient peoples who built sacred sites over them.

life-force energy. Energy that is all around us in nature and that is emitted by the earth.

light body. Energetic body; the quality of energy around a person, as opposed to their physical body. See MerKaBa.

matter. Patterns of energy we perceive as having substance.

medicine. The inherent power within all things.

medicine wheel. A Native American system of prayer, meditation and discovery, recognizing that life follows a circle. The wheel's directions and their significance, concepts from which all things are said to derive, include east (newness, discovery), south (youth, growth, healing), west (introspection, setting sun, light within), north (wisdom, elders, ancestors), center (soul, spirit), above (Heavenly Father), and below (Earth Mother).

meridians. Lines along the body where energy is channeled; often used in acupuncture and other energy medicine to effect healing.

MerKaBa. In sacred geometry, a star tetrahedron; an energetic framework that forms a blueprint for spirit to attach and from which, in plants and animals, DNA creates a physical expression; a geometric form that includes the light body; a pattern of energy shared by animals, plants, stones and all objects, including those that are man-made.

mind of God. Expansion of human thought to higher consciousness as far as is conceivable.

morphogenic field. A universal field encoding the basic pattern of an object. From the Greek morphe, which means form, and genesis, which denotes coming into being. Non-corporeal beings manifest in three-dimensional reality through morphogenic resonance.

nagual. In Toltec shamanism, what is really real (non-ordinary reality), as opposed to what we think is real according to our consensus reality; everything that can be. See tonal.

native peoples. Indigenous cultures practicing traditional nature-based ways.

non-ordinary reality. Reality as seen when everyday constraints and predispositions are eliminated through trance or other methods.

personality. All that we adhere to, or believe, that makes us who we think we are. See ego.

pipe fast. See vision quest.

portal. A vortex through which objects and entities can pass from one dimension of reality to another while realm shifting.

power animal. An animal that offers guidance and protection; a totem.

power song, or heart song. A song that expresses the unique, positive energies, traits, and intents of an individual, usually discovered through fasting and prayer.

power spot. A place where all energies of a structure or tract of land are focused.

prana. Universal life-force energy.

prayer stick. A stick, either ornate or plain, that has been consecrated through prayer; wrapped with cloth, ribbon, or yarn; and most often, planted in the ground to carry a prayer.

rattling. Shaking a rattle to break up energy or bring in energy.

realm shifting. The movement of objects between dimensions; while some objects, such as quartz crystals, do this routinely because of their energetic composition, others will disappear and reappear only when near a portal.

Reiki. A Japanese form of energy medicine involving sacred symbols and guides; use of the hands to channel healing energy.

sacred circle. All beings in our lives — past, present and future — who are connected to us; consecrated circle for ceremony.

self-talk. The inner dialogue inside our minds; the "what ifs," "buts," judgments and fears that prevent us from being who we really are.

shaman. Siberian word meaning "one who sees in the dark"; a person who uses earth energy, guides, and power animals for insight; a medicine man or woman.

shielding. Creating an intentional protective energy layer around you to deflect external negative energy.

shift of the ages. Powerful changes in energy patterns now occurring on earth as a prelude to earth transformations and humanity's eventual development of higher consciousness.

skan. Lakota word, meaning power of the wind; a sacred force of movement; that which existed before God; life-force energy; the principle that manifests prayers from prayer flags.

smudging. Burning a plant such as sage, cedar or sweetgrass to purify the energy of an area.

soul. The essential life force, or essence, of a being that is eternal from lifetime to lifetime.

soul retrieval. The act of retrieving soul parts, or essence, lost through trauma or stolen by another individual.

space. Any defined area, including the objects within it.

spiral of ascension. Spiral of life that offers a changing perspective as new lessons are encountered and old ones repeated, until the lessons are finally learned.

spirit. The essential quality of a being as an expression of soul; non-corporeal aspect of a person aligned their with soul purpose.

spirit quest. Following only what spirit dictates, usually over the course of days.

star beings. Beings from the stars whom cultures around the globe and throughout time have claimed influenced human development and are honored at some sacred spots.

Stillpoint. An inner place of total silence and stillness, where intuition and creativity originate and balance can be found; the source of being.

tesseract. A hypercube, also called the 8-cell or octachoron; sacred geometry shape for ceremony, frequently depicted in art as the shape of angels.

thought forms. Organized patterns of energy, either free-floating or embedded in a space, that can be broken up by rattling or other means of transmutation.

tonal. In Toltec shamanism, the idea of what is real (our common, consensus reality), in contrast to what is really real (non-ordinary reality), the nagual. See nagual.

transmutation. Changing energy from one state to another, such as transforming water to ice or vapor and vice versa; changing negative, or inert, energy into positive, or active, energy; or neutralizing energy to be reabsorbed by the earth. Ancient practices involved burying an energized object in the ground, burning it with fire or submerging it in water.

umane. (Lakota: OO-Mah-ne) Sacred symbol of Earth energy in its raw form, often depicted in stone pictographs as a square with lines of energy from each corner, or as a square with elongated corners to represent power coming from and going out to all corners of the universe.

unoli (You-Know-Lee). Cherokee, meaning literally "winds" but used as a designation for the powers of the directions.

vibrational rate/vibrational frequency. The measurable level of energy of a person, place or object; the higher the rate, the closer to the source, or optimal wholeness.

vision quest. A period of time spent in a desolate or isolated spot under the tutelage of a spiritual elder, intended as an opportunity for discovering the inner self, the meaning of life or to connect with higher beings.

vortexes. Doorways or portals into other dimensions; areas where energy in flux can affect time and space.

wakan. Lakota word meaning "sacred."

Wakan-Tanka. Lakota word for Great Spirit, or the Great Mystery, God.

wand. A long, thin implement used to direct energy when pointed. Some are ornate, with carvings, feathers, beads and similar adornments, while others are as simple as a twig or a feather.

wild spirit. A spirit of the land that usually inhabits wilderness areas away from civilization or contact with humans; ally.

will of creation. Energy of the moment, moving from one state to another; the potential to transform to another manifestation.

Bibliography

Andrews, Ted. *Animal-Speak: The Spiritual and Magical Powers of Creatures Great and Small*. St. Paul, Minn: Llewellyn Publications, 1998.

———. *Animal-Wise: The Spirit Language and Signs of Nature*. St. Paul, Minn.: Llewellyn Publications, 1999.

Backster, Cleve. *Primary Perception: Biocommunication with Plants, Living Foods, and Human Cells*. Anza, Calif.: White Rose Millennium Press, 2003.

Bird, Chris and Thompkins, Peter. *Secret Life of Plants*. New York: Harper Paperbacks, 1989.

Boyd, Doug. *Mad Bear: Spirit, Healing, and the Sacred in the Life of a Native American Medicine Man*. New York: Touchstone, 1994.

Byrne, Rhonda. *The Secret*. New York: Simon and Schuster, 2006.

Carroll, Lewis. *Through The Looking-Glass*. Austin, Texas: 1st World Library, 2004.

Castaneda, Carlos. *Journey To Ixtlan: The Lessons of Don Juan*. New York: Simon and Schuster, 1977.

———. *The Teachings of Don Juan: A Yaqui Way of Knowledge*. New York: Ballantine,

Dyer, Wayne W. *The Power of Intention*. Carlsbad, Calif.: Hay House, 2004.

Dove, Mourning. *Coyote Stories*. Lincoln and London, Neb.: University of Nebraska Press, 1990.

Eagle Feather, Ken. *A Toltec Path*. Charlottesville, VA: Hampton Roads, 1995.

Emoto, Masaru. *The Message from Water*, vols. 1 and 2. Tokyo, Japan: Hado Kyoikusha, 2004.

Ewing, Jim PathFinder. *Clearing: A Guide to Liberating Energies Trapped in Buildings and Lands*. Findhorn, Scotland: Findhorn Press, 2006.

———. Jim PathFinder. *Finding Sanctuary in Nature: Simple Ceremonies in the Native American Tradition of Healing Yourself and Others*. Findhorn, Scotland: Findhorn Press, 2007.

Gerber, Richard, M.D. *Vibrational Medicine: New Choices for Healing Ourselves*. Santa Fe, N.M.: Bear and Company, 1996.

Harner, Michael. *The Way of the Shaman*. New York: Harper, 1980.

Hawkins, David R., M.D., Ph.D. *Power vs. Force: The Hidden Determinants of Human Behavior*. Carlsbad, Calif.: Hay House, 1995.

Ingerman, Sandra. *Medicine for the Earth: How to Transform Personal and Environmental Toxins*. New York: Three Rivers Press, 2000.

———. *Shamanic Journeying: A Beginner's Guide*. Boulder, CO: Sounds True, 2004.

———. *Soul Retrieval: Mending the Fragmented Self*. San Francisco: Harper, 1991.

———. *Welcome Home: Following Your Soul's Journey Home*. San Francisco: Harper, 1993.

Laszlo, Ervin. *Science and the Akashic Field: An Integral Theory of Everything*. Rochester, Vt.: Inner Traditions, 2004.

L'Engle, Madeleine. *A Wrinkle in Time*. New York: Farrar, Straus and Giroux, 1962.

Mann, Charles C. *1491: New Revelations of the Americas Before Columbus*. New York: Knopf, 2005.

Medicine Eagle, Brooke. *The Last Ghost Dance: A Guide for Earth Mages*. New York: Wellspring/Ballantine, 2000.

———. *Buffalo Woman Comes Singing*. New York: Ballantine Books, 1991.

Melchizedek, Drunvalo. *Ancient Secrets of the Flower of Life,* vols. 1 and 2. Flagstaff, AZ: Light Technology Publishing, 1990.

Bibliography

Melody. *Love Is In The Earth: A kaleidoscope of Crystals.* Wheat Ridge, Colo.: Earth-Love Publishing House, Ltd., 1995.

Moore, Christopher. *Coyote Blue.* New York: HarperCollins, 2004.

Neihardt, John G. *Black Elk Speaks: Being the Life Story of a Holy Man of the Oglala Sioux.* Lincoln: University of Nebraska Press, 2000.

Peterson, Roger Tory, ed. *A Field Guide to Medicinal Plants and Herbs: Of Eastern and Central North America.* Boston: Houghton Mifflin Company, 1999.

——. *A Field Guide to Edible Wild Plants: Eastern and Central North America.* Boston: Houghton Mifflin Company, 1999.

Ruiz, Don Miguel. *The Four Agreements.* San Rafael, CA: Amber-Allen Publishing, 1997.

Sams, Jamie. *Dancing the Dream: The Seven Sacred Paths of Human Transformation.* New York: HarperCollins, 1998.

Steiner, Rudolf. *The Fourth Dimension: Sacred Geometry, Alchemy, and Mathematics.* Great Barrington, Mass.: Anthroposophic Press, 2001.

Sheldrake, Rupert. *A New Science of Life.* Los Angeles: J P Tarcher, 1982.

Wilson, Edward O. *Biophilia: The Human Bond with Other Species.* Boston: Harvard University Press, 1986.

Ywahoo, Dhyani. *Voices of the Ancestors: Cherokee Teachings from the Wisdom Fire.* Boston: Shambhala Publications, 1987.

About the Author

Jim PathFinder Ewing (Nvnehi Awatisgi) is a Reiki Master teacher who also teaches shamanism in Lena, Mississippi, where he lives with his wife, Annette Waya Ewing. He travels extensively, giving workshops, classes and lectures, and is available for consultation. To receive a schedule of workshops he teaches or sponsors, please write to:

> Jim PathFinder Ewing
> P.O. Box 387
> Lena, MS 39094

To subscribe to his free monthly online newsletter, *Keeping in Touch,* visit his Web site, Healing the Earth/Ourselves, at http://www.blueskywaters.com.